PRAISE FOR
Why Not God?

If, in this mixed up and conflicted world in which we live, you are trying to work out what it is that you believe and why you believe it, then *Why Not God?* is the book for you! With clarity and insight, and a good deal of common sense, Charles Mastroni will help you examine your beliefs, clarify what is true and not so true, and shape a healthy worldview with God at the center.

—Rev. Paul McPheeters, New England Regional Pastor for the Conservative Congregational Christian Conference

The world is fast-paced, complex and confusing. Just to make it through the day with its obligations and many distractions keeps us from focusing on ultimate questions, such as, "Why not God?" This book provides an opportunity to think about beliefs and where they come from. The busyness of life often leads us to adopt beliefs and worldviews that are absorbed but not carefully examined. In *Why Not God?*, Charles Mastroni explains how he has come to believe and hold a Reformed Christian worldview, while challenging the reader to examine their own beliefs with the same honesty. Anyone on a quest for truth will be helped by this fine book.

—Rev. Richard H. Woodward, retired Congregational church pastor

Why Not God? is a compelling read. For as long as I have known Charles Mastroni he has been burdened to have others enjoy the blessing of knowing the only true God through the Lord Jesus Christ. Read carefully (with pen in hand), learn deeply, and your mind and heart will be challenged.

—Rev. Jim Beddows, retired pastor

WHY NOT GOD?

Rethinking Our Beliefs
About Truth and Faith

WHY NOT GOD?

Rethinking Our Beliefs About Truth and Faith

CHARLES MASTRONI

EMERALD LAKE
BOOKS
Sherman, Connecticut

Library of Congress Cataloging-in-Publication Data

Names: Mastroni, Charles, 1954- author

Title: Why not God?: Rethinking our beliefs about truth and faith/by
  Charles Mastroni.

Description: Sherman: Emerald Lake Books, [2026] | Includes
  appendixes. | Includes bibliographical references.

Identifiers: LCCN 2026006736 (print) | LCCN 2026006737 (ebook) |
  ISBN 9781945847905 paperback | ISBN 9781945847912 epub

Subjects: LCSH: Faith (Christianity) | Secularism | Truthfulness and
  falsehood--Religious aspects--Christianity

Classification: LCC BV4637 .M34 2026 (print) | LCC BV4637 (ebook)

LC record available at https://lccn.loc.gov/2026006736

LC ebook record available at https://lccn.loc.gov/2026006737

To all the pastors and mentors who taught me over the years. I hope you know what a blessing you have been to me and all your congregations.

Rev. Dr. Patrick Novack

Rev. Randy Thompson

Rev. Dr. Mark Horton

Rev. Paul Astbury

Rev. Jim Beddows

Rev. Richard Woodward

Rev. Dr. Bernie Powell

CONTENTS

Author's Note

Have you ever wondered what's gone wrong in our world—or in your own heart? Many people today feel lost, unsure of what to believe, or even who they really are. We search for truth in science, politics or personal experience, yet the deeper questions still remain: *Why am I here? What's the purpose of my life? Is there more beyond this world?*

This book began as my own search for meaning. I lived through the cultural revolutions of the 1960s and '70s, a time of great change, freedom and confusion. Like many, I chased after ideas and pleasures that promised fulfillment but left me empty. In that emptiness, I asked God for meaning, and he answered. What began as curiosity became faith, and that faith has transformed my life ever since.

Over the years, I've come to see how profoundly our beliefs shape not only who we are but also the societies we build. Whether or not we recognize it, every one of us lives out a worldview—a framework that answers life's biggest questions about God, humanity, truth, morality and what happens after death. When that framework is distorted or missing altogether, confusion follows. We lose our sense of identity and direction, and our world reflects that loss.

I felt compelled to write this book because so many people today see God as just one option among many, or they've dismissed him altogether. Yet I've come to believe that faith in God isn't just one option. It's the *best* option for understanding ourselves and the world around us. Knowing our Creator provides a foundation strong enough to build both a meaningful life and a healthy society.

Another reason for writing is deeply personal. Many people I care about don't believe in God. My faith has brought me peace, hope and purpose, and I want others, especially those I love, to know that same joy. I believe eternal life is real, and I long for everyone to share in it. For those who already know God, I hope these pages deepen your understanding and strengthen your confidence in him.

In *Why Not God?* we'll explore the contrast between two major worldviews: one that leaves God out of the picture and another (the Christian worldview) that places him at the center. Using a simple framework, we'll look at what we believe about God, humanity, truth, morality and our ultimate destiny. Along the way, we'll also examine the modern "idols" that compete for our faith and attention—things like progress, pleasure and personal autonomy— and see how they measure up against the truth of Scripture.

This isn't an academic argument or a sermon. It's an invitation to think deeply and honestly about what you believe and why. Whether you're skeptical, curious or already a believer, my hope is that this book helps you see the world, and yourself, more clearly through God's eyes.

I invite you to come with an open mind and a willing heart. Ask questions. Reflect. Challenge your assumptions. And as you do, consider this simple but life-changing question: *Why Not God?*

Charles Mastroni
March 2026

Part One. Foundational Wisdom

CHAPTER 1

The Formation of Worldviews

Do you know God? Or are you unsure if he's even real? If you aren't certain, why aren't you? The way we come to know what we know and believe what we believe is shaped by many things. Deep inside each of us is a unique self, shaped over time, hidden beneath the many roles we play—child, sibling, friend, parent, employee, boss. That self acquired an array of beliefs and a knowledge of what is true that has shaped our lives in the deepest sense. It wears these like a set of clothes to face life.

But how do we come to develop these viewpoints—and have you ever stopped to ask whether what you believe is really true? This book examines how beliefs shape us individually, as well as the cultures we live in.

Some of the questions we will address include:

- Does God exist?
- What is humankind?
- Where does knowledge come from?
- What is right and wrong?
- Is there life after death?

The TAKES Model

When studying belief systems, many scholars use a classic model that involves breaking a worldview down into five key areas and exploring them individually. This is called the "TAKES model" because it covers the theology, anthropology, knowledge, ethics—which includes morals—and salvation of a culture. (Notice that the questions above each correlate to one of these key areas.)

I have used this same model as the framework for this book because it is not only suitable for studying a culture, but it can also be used to understand one's own worldview.

But first, let's look at what each of these key areas refers to.

- **Theology:** beliefs about the existence and character of God

- **Anthropology:** beliefs dealing with the origin, essence and destiny of humans

- **Knowledge:** beliefs about the foundation and source of understanding

- **Ethics:** beliefs about the nature of right and wrong

- **Salvation:** beliefs about the power and consequences of sin and our deliverance from it

Our worldview is made up of what we believe to be true about the world, ourselves and others. It is the basis of how we live and the choices we make. The civilizations we grow up in, as well as our personal histories, also shape our worldviews. Historically, cultures have been molded primarily by the major religions. However, since the Age of Enlightenment in 1685, science has had an ever-increasing influence on our beliefs. As a result, many people don't believe in anything spiritual and rely only on what rational thought can explain.

But even worldviews that do not include religion still include theology (the claim that there is no God, which is in itself a theology). Religions and Darwin's theory of evolution also address anthropology. Most faiths cover creation as part of the origin of the universe, and science has the Big Bang theory. The same thing applies when it comes to the nature and destiny of humans. Both religion and science address these questions.

As to ethics, the norms of right and wrong and good and evil are typically culturally based and influenced by religions. Sciences like psychology somewhat address right and wrong, but psychology views morality as a product of human nature rather than divine will.

Science-based worldviews have no objective basis for ethics other than what is acceptable in a culture, which can be substantially influenced by politics and governments. Individual scientists may have a set of values and ethics, but the field itself offers no clear set of morals, even though the governments that fund them impose laws that reflect the morals of their culture.

Religious worldviews include a framework for salvation and the afterlife. However, worldviews based on science do not believe in salvation or life after death. Individual scientists have their own ideas regarding the afterlife, but the field of science itself is silent on this topic.

I am not an expert scientist, nor do I know every philosophy, nor am I an expert in every religion. I am more concerned with how all these influences shape people's thoughts and feelings and how they practically affect our lives, souls and world. Most people are not experts in any of the above fields either, yet we all have a sense of right and wrong, what we believe is true, and what we value.

Worldviews and Influences

Our worldview comes from somewhere and exists in our psyche, so we should understand what influences us. Common sense, although it sometimes seems scarce, plays a part in our view of reality and should not be disregarded.

Experts, scientists and scholars tend to focus on their specialized knowledge and assume it is the most prevalent and important, often at the expense of other theories and sound judgment. If they do not challenge the status quo, they have nothing new to offer. In a drive to publish some new truth, they can break the bounds of wisdom and accepted truth. They need to publish or perish in academia, to shock and be controversial to sell books, to keep current with all the other experts, and to ride the waves of the latest and greatest controversial ideas. Often, their careers matter more than the truth when seeking funding. These factors tend to skew perspectives, conclusions and common sense, and they vigorously promote their ideas, frequently to the detriment of the public.

> Good sense is not so common.
> Wisdom is never so scant,
> As when experts selling their theories
> go on their favorite rants.

> True foundations they must challenge
> with new knowledge, so they claim.
> Pushing out traditional wisdom
> so they can make themselves a name.

> Too many fools with a PhD
> have new truths to peddle to you and me.

Worldviews produce truth or falsehood and hope or hopelessness, resulting in shaping people's minds and hearts. A nonreligious worldview produces a very different mindset than a religious one. Therefore, conflicting perspectives produce very different people, societies and cultures, affecting the quality of life both individually and corporately. Essentially, our worldview defines what we consider to be true when we hear new information, and we trust sources that already agree with our viewpoint.

Mass media has a major influence on our worldviews: news, movies, television and the ever-present social media. Headlines report groundbreaking scientific studies, typically accompanied by brief statements or summaries, but since most people are not experts in these fields, the overwhelming majority of the population never reads the premises or details of the studies themselves.

The general public is not familiar with the methodology of stating and evaluating a hypothesis, nor is it proficient in the statistical analysis that accompanies many studies. As a result, mass media sources can skew perceptions via headlines, sound bites, and storylines in movies or on television. This means consumers only get a general impression of knowledge, which leads to a false or incomplete truth. The political bent of the reporting sources can also slant the perspectives of the public. With this in mind, many of the references in this book are not from scholarly journals but from news sources, websites, and cultural references because these are what actually influence worldviews.

From the 1970s onward, especially in Western popular culture, religion in general and Christianity in particular have not been held in high regard by progressive thinkers. When I refer to the terms *progressive thought* and *progressivism* in this book, I mean the modern movement that promotes social reform through human reason and evolving moral standards, often emphasizing personal autonomy and social justice, rather than the progressivism of the early twentieth century, which focused mainly on economic fairness, religious liberties, and political reform.

Religion: A Myth or the Truth?

I trust that if you are reading this book, you probably have the integrity, common sense and intelligence to know the wisdom and truth found in religious teachings have benefited humankind. Yes, those same teachings have been misused to foment wars and other atrocities, but only in the pursuit of personal power. A fair-minded perspective should also acknowledge that religions began with the goal of bringing goodness and truth to humanity.

They shape the moral character of cultures and worldviews and, therefore, individuals as well.

People commonly discount the Bible and any wisdom it contains, primarily because they consider the notion of God to be antiquated, believing we have evolved past a need for him. Many don't even consider it possible that God exists, and some academics call all religions myths. In their view, science is the only authority of truth. The problem with this belief is that science offers no moral foundation for living life or understanding the difference between right and wrong. These have historically come from religions, and they have had enough positive influence over time for civilizations to exist and even flourish. Science offers nothing in this regard.

Institutions consist of imperfect men and women. Hopefully, you realize there may be truth to the Christian faith in God despite the fallible people who practice it. The presence of human limitations doesn't imply the absence of truth in religions. It just means that no perfect people regularly practice a religion without corruption creeping in to some degree.

An honest reading of history from the Middle Ages to the present shows Western culture was predominantly shaped by Christian thought and a belief in God, and, secondarily, by Greek philosophical thought passed down through traditional education. This influence has produced minds like Isaac Newton, Johann Sebastian Bach, Leonardo DaVinci, Albert Einstein, William Shakespeare, William of Occam, Thomas Aquinas, and Augustine of Hippo, among others. Christians and Christian churches primarily founded the great universities in the West[1] and promoted education for everyone as much as possible. Christian theology was primarily taught there. Local churches established community schools to teach reading, math, science, literature and the Christian religion. Most of these great universities have left their Christian

---

[1] "Pathways of Development," *Christianity Studies*, Wesleyan University, accessed August 18, 2025, charlesmastroni.com/universities.

roots and have become progressively secular since the Age of Enlightenment.

Historically, church attendance and public school education also included God in the United States. Christianity was the primary influence in Western culture until the mid-twentieth century, when it was removed from American schools. It was not a perfect system, but it was the way things were.

Unfortunately, many atrocities have been perpetrated by the church. But this is because of the misuse of religion, the way Islam has been misused to produce terrorists. The social activism of global warming results in young minds that destroy classic artworks. Nazi propaganda promoted the antisemitism that led to the mass slaughter of Jewish people. Worldviews do hold this kind of power. Another example is the perversion of the revolutionary movement of the 1960s by groups like the Weathermen (later known as the Weather Underground), who ended up being domestic terrorists and bombing government buildings.[2]

The misuse of any religion results from our fallen human nature, the same as any other tainted ideology. Our very flawed selves tend to conform religious teachings to the self-serving pursuit of personal power, believing the end justifies the means. That is not how religious founders meant for their teachings to be followed.

The Primary Source of Worldviews

As imperfect as institutional faiths are, historically, religions are the primary source of worldviews, foundational wisdom and truth in our cultures. Hinduism has influenced India. Shinto and Buddhism have influenced Japan. Islam has influenced the Arab-speaking world. And Christianity has influenced Western culture.

Even secular reactions to religions are based on an automatic rejection of religious truth and an attempt to disprove it, much like

---

[2] "History: Weather Underground Bombings," FBI.gov, accessed January 8, 2026, charlesmastroni.com/underground.

a teenager trying to prove their parents wrong. Secular worldviews compete with religious worldviews for what is considered true and moral in any given culture.

Even with fallible humans, the moral teachings of religions have created values in our cultures that keep us from complete anarchy and self-destruction. Most faith-based worldviews enable societies to exist by condemning murder, theft, adultery, and other uncivilized acts, and they promote ideals like solid family structure, fairness to strangers, truth-telling, justice and other moral behavior.

Throughout history, religions have been a primary factor in shaping cultures and, therefore, our core beings. They hit where we live in our psyche—our inner self, which is the seat of memory, desire, conscience, emotion and will—what Scripture traditionally calls the soul. Religions also shape what we believe to be true, and what we believe determines how we live.

CHAPTER 2

The Power of Belief

Why can't I believe whatever I want? This seems to be the attitude of most people these days. While you can believe anything you want, is what you believe true? Is it good for your life? A person can convince themselves of anything: true or false, helpful or harmful. We can be swayed by what our culture believes is truth, by people we know, and by other influences. We can also be persuaded something is true (even if it's false) simply because it's what we strongly desire.

However, our beliefs have consequences. Once they take root in our minds, they lead us along a path of thought toward an inevitable way of living and acting, much like a train on a track. Here is my answer to the question "Why can't I believe whatever I want?" When you believe in something that is not true, real and good, you are letting falsehoods guide your life. Let's look at some very practical examples.

Many young children believe they can drive a car, when in reality, they can't. They don't know how, can't reach the pedals, can't see over the steering wheel, and don't understand the rules of the road. If they were to try to drive, they would have an accident, get hurt, and possibly harm others too.

This would be like living your life according to a belief that is not true, good or right. Your life, like a car, would be out of control, damaging you and others. However, if you believe you can drive a car and you actually have the skills and knowledge to do so, you will most likely drive safely.

The same holds true for flying an aircraft. If you don't know how to fly a plane and you believe you can, well, you know the result.

Building a house is another example. You must have the right tools and know-how to use the proper materials and construct a solid structure that doesn't leak and can withstand the weather. If you truly know how to connect the wiring, install the furnace, etc., you can build a house successfully. If you believe you have what you need to be successful, but actually lack the necessary familiarity and understanding of these concepts, your structure will fail. You might even be electrocuted, and the house could burn down.

It is the same with our lives, hearts and minds. Believing truth is living in reality, and believing falsehoods is living in fantasy, which does not produce good results.

Many people believe drugs and alcohol are fun—that they are the answer to acceptance from others, an escape from problems, freedom from inhibitions, or just feel too good to pass up. If they continue to indulge this belief, then they risk addiction and possibly an overdose, a car crash, a job loss, a criminal lifestyle, or worse. When someone believes drugs and alcohol are not the answer to what they're looking for, they eliminate these risks.

If a person holds that worldly success is the most important pursuit in life and they seek meaning solely from work and money, they will be disappointed and even crushed if they don't achieve their goals or get laid off. In the same manner, if someone believes the most important achievement in their life is their marriage and family, they will be devastated if they are the victim of a cheating spouse or a rebellious teen. While success and a healthy marriage are wonderful and meaningful parts of life, if they are the only metrics for a successful life, then a person is defeated when they fail. As important as these are, they are not completely reliable as the source of our ultimate purpose.

It is of utmost importance that we believe and trust in what is true, real and good, especially when it comes to our core beliefs, which are the foundation of our psyche and the basis for the decisions we make. As such, our beliefs need to be grounded in reality, or we cannot successfully navigate life's challenges. Truth forms a solid core in a person that is not easily shaken or swayed by falsehoods, other people, or the trials we face in this imperfect world.

> Believe what you will,
> you are certainly free.
>
> God made it that way
> for humanity.
>
> What is true leads to blessing,
> a foundation dug deep.
>
> What is false leads to failure,
> and eyes that will weep.
>
> You will live with the effects
> of what you hold true.
>
> Wise folks from the past
> have left wisdom for you.
>
> Seek wisdom and truth,
> in old age and youth.

As important as it is for us to evaluate our beliefs, we rarely do so. Instead, we usually just trust they are valid without question. As a matter of fact, we assess everything we see and hear based on what we think is true, including other people, history, current events, relationships, situations, decisions and actions we should take. How did you come to believe what you believe? Have you ever considered this for yourself?

What you believe or disbelieve about God seriously affects your worldview and actions. Using the TAKES model, if your belief is that God exists and he cares what you do (your theology), then you will act differently, make different decisions, and see the world differently than a person who doesn't believe he exists or cares. This, in turn, affects how you view your fellow humans. Believing in the God who created us puts us all on an equal footing when we see each other; every person has value because he made them.

This anthropology differs greatly from that of the theory of evolution, which evaluates people by their genetic superiority to determine who is most fit to reproduce. Talented people are more valued than nontalented individuals, as evidenced by the amount of money (value) paid to athletes and celebrities.

Likewise, your theology and anthropology, or what you believe about God and people, will determine what you accept as knowledge or wisdom. Where does knowledge come from: God or human beings? Is there a superior mind than that of people? (I certainly hope so!) And who determines ethics and morality: a superior God or our culture? Finally, is there salvation and an afterlife? If there is, what is our eternal fate and who determines it?

All the things we believe, as categorized using the TAKES model, are interconnected and profoundly impactful in shaping our worldview and, therefore, ourselves.

An examination of the word *belief* is in order here. Let's take a look at a couple of definitions:

1. According to Merriam-Webster, belief is an acceptance that a statement is true or that something exists. It can also be something one accepts as true or real, a religious conviction, and trust, faith or confidence in someone or something.[3] Therefore, belief and truth are connected to reality and existence. This includes religious and nonreligious beliefs.

2. According to an article by Ralph Lewis, MD, in *Psychology Today*, "Beliefs are our brain's way of making sense of

---

[3] *Merriam-Webster Dictionary*, "belief," accessed January 8, 2026, charlesmastroni.com/belief.

and navigating our complex world. They are mental representations of the ways our brains expect things in our environment to behave, and how things should be related to each other—the patterns our brain expects the world to conform to. Beliefs are templates for efficient learning and are often essential for survival."[4] Our beliefs assess new information, experiences, facts and even the beliefs of others. We do judge others, whether we admit it or not. Everyone considers people who do not agree with them to be wrong and people who agree with them to be right. And the phrase "how our brains expect things to be in our environment" recognizes that our beliefs are also what we expect the world to be or should be. And our actions are based on them.

How Our Beliefs Are Formed

Beliefs exist in the mind. But where do they come from, and how do they form? Here is an admittedly brief overview. Beliefs are formed when the individual's unique self interacts and learns from outside stimuli. A wholly separate being is in that little body, with a will and wants. Every newborn is not a completely blank slate. Each baby is an individual with a unique personality and traits that develop as they grow and experience the world around them. Physically, we are all unique—even identical twins don't share the same fingerprints.[5]

Additionally, a living spirit is in a newborn. This is what makes an infant alive versus a stillborn baby. A stillborn's physical body may be fully developed, but it is not alive in this world. Yet, in a

---

[4] Ralph Lewis, MD, "What Actually Is a Belief? And Why Is It So Hard to Change?," *Psychology Today*, October 7, 2018, charlesmastroni.com/beliefchange.
[5] Kristeen Cherney, "Why Twins Don't Have Identical Fingerprints," Healthline, May 30, 2023, charlesmastroni.com/twins.

newborn, an individual with their corresponding unique spirit lives in the body.

While the spirit of a person is invisible, as are their thoughts and emotions, it shows its qualities physically. We can certainly see how thoughts and emotions are expressed through our bodies. They are reflected on our faces and communicated through our actions. However, they are invisible by themselves.

Knowledge and beliefs are learned and acquired as soon as life begins, through interactions with the environment. At the earliest stage of life, children are born with no beliefs that we know of. The body functions instinctively. We do not will ourselves into existence, nor do we know how to construct our bodies or bring about our own lives. Even basic functions, like seeing with our eyes or hearing with our ears, are not acts under our conscious control. Our bodies are formed from forces outside our individual selves.

Even though the body knows how to eat, cry, eliminate waste, sleep and wake up, this biological knowledge does not by itself create beliefs and worldviews. Eventually, the child's mind explores movement, senses and experiences using sensory input that comes from outside the child. With practice, the child learns how to focus their eyes and move their limbs as they begin exploring their body. They learn the comforting touch, faces and voices of their parents, which leads them to bond with, believe and recognize their mom and dad.

The inner being of the child (in other words, their individuality) learns, knows and believes what exists around them through their senses. They develop likes and dislikes, and they express them definitively in their tastes for various foods, toys and even preferences for favorite people. By trial and error, a child learns to feed themselves, crawl and walk. They develop speech and learn the meanings of words, like *water, mom* and *dad*. They learn that siblings are brothers and sisters. This is knowledge that the child acquires and believes to be true. As time goes on, more knowledge is gained and believed: fire is hot, ice is cold, dogs can bite, cats can scratch, bumping the head hurts, and so on. This is a practical set of genuine beliefs.

In addition, the parents teach behavioral expectations: not to hit or bite, to consider others, to share, to tell the truth, to not run into the street, to respect teachers, to learn to read, and so forth. We are talking about the basic truth of what is right and wrong—of good and bad behavior—that children learn through the socialization process. And kids see what parents and others do as well, and they imitate and assimilate it. Again, these are all influences outside of the child.

However, children may reject expectations for their behavior based on what they want. A child may be taught to share, but they may or may not do so, depending on what they desire. The same holds true for lying versus telling the truth. That doesn't mean they disagree that sharing and telling the truth are the right thing to do, it's just that they may not *want* to share or tell the truth, exercising their willfulness, as the case may be.

In this book, we cannot examine all behaviors and compare them to beliefs. Suffice it to say that, fundamentally, a child learns and trusts what they see and are taught. This input comes from outside them, and then they incorporate it into themselves as a belief.

The real change in the nature of beliefs comes when a child reaches the age of reason at around seven years old. This is when they start to understand ideas as concepts of abstract thought and imagine situations hypothetically (although this skill is not fully developed until around age twelve).[6] Children already hold many fundamental beliefs at this age. They can weigh one idea against another and choose one way of being versus another. They can understand new ideas and concepts that go beyond their earlier, simpler ways of thinking—but these are still largely connected to what they already believe and know. At this point, their orientation to their environment reflects a developing worldview based on

---

[6] Kendra Cherry, "Piaget's 4 Stages of Cognitive Development Explained," *Verywell Mind*, updated November 13, 2025, charlesmastroni.com/piaget.

their experiences so far. But this perspective is less fixed for a child than an adult, since a young person is more malleable and easily influenced.

New knowledge and experiences can sometimes change a person's core convictions, but this doesn't happen often. What usually happens is that we reject anything new that doesn't align with our existing worldview. However, when new ideas shape our understanding, this is the nurture side (the environment) of the nature versus nurture debate. In this circumstance, individuals adjust their worldview as they evaluate environmental influences, such as new ideas or knowledge.

On the nature side, an individual interacts uniquely with their environment. As a result, their response to it can differ drastically from person to person. We see this in families where a healthy environment teaches right from wrong, but one of the children grows up to be a criminal.

A person can want something different from what they are taught and even from what they believe to be right. For example, someone can be told stealing is wrong and even have honest parents and siblings who don't steal, but they want something badly enough to take it. And they will try to conceal their theft because they know it is unacceptable. If they didn't believe that, they wouldn't try to hide the deed.

Society says murder is wrong, rape is wrong, child molestation is wrong, and theft is wrong, among many other things. Virtually everyone believes these actions are morally unethical. However, the individual offender wants what they want more than any restraint of society (their environment) or their own conscience. They think they can get away with it. Or they convince themselves they have to fulfill this desire. This allows them to justify their actions in their minds. The lesson here is that strong desires do not equate to true and good beliefs.

Some individuals grow up in a terrible environment, yet turn out to be an upstanding person of high character. In this case, there is a rejection of so-called truths, which are actually lessons from a bad environment, and they choose to be good to their fellow people, regardless of how they were raised. They willingly adhere to the true and healthy standards of society and their conscience, believing what is good and real. Making such choices results in a high-character individual. This reflects the nature side of the equation, where our temperament and predispositions come into play. As previously seen, the individual can also reject a good environment (nurture) and become amoral. It is the individual who makes choices and holds beliefs.

In summary, beliefs are formed when an individual's nature learns from their nurturing environment and are based on what they accept as true and real. When we hit the age of reason at age seven, we begin to weigh new information from outside ourselves and compare it to our existing beliefs, making adjustments as we deem necessary. Yet, their formation is more complex after the age of reason and is influenced by the person's desires and insights regarding what to accept as true. Minds can adapt based on new knowledge, information and experiences, but they are incorporated or rejected based on existing beliefs. This shapes our worldviews as well as ourselves because our choices and individuality are intimately tied to what we hold to be true.

Yet throughout the process, we do not invent truth. We discover it. We do not invent beliefs. We discern things to be true or false, right or wrong, good or bad, harmful or helpful. This is the key takeaway: our beliefs result from what we encounter outside ourselves. Even the words we use reflect this. When we come to believe or know something, we *realize* it. It is a *realization* of a truth and, therefore, a belief that it is real. Taking a truth into our minds and believing it is like taking food into our bodies—it becomes part of our core self.

> We take in knowledge, false or true,
> what we believe becomes part of me and you.
>
> Our minds are built on what we believe,
> a house that's strong or one that's diseased.
>
> A foundation of truth will last through life's storms,
> a house built on lies will not last long.
>
> Our minds are made by beliefs
> as our bodies are fed by food.
>
> Lies will make you sick
> while the truth will do you good.

Why Beliefs Are So Important

Like a train rolling down the tracks, our beliefs lead to our decisions and actions unless we come to believe something new. The repeated choices and actions instill patterns of thoughts, feelings and reactions, and these are recorded in the physical brain and nervous system as we respond to events and experiences. We are an integrated mind, body and spirit working intimately with each other, inseparably. We tend to think of these three as separate in Western culture. However, the reality is they are united as one.

These ingrained patterns end up shaping the quality of our lives—this is inevitable. Over time, our beliefs become part of our subconscious, and we do not question them very often—that is just who we are, and we simply react.[7] Beliefs are integral to our identity and how we view ourselves and the world.

Making a significant change requires instilling a new belief to trigger it. These transitions result from a shift in our beliefs about:

- who God is [theology].

- who we are or should be as a person [anthropology].

---

[7] Psychologs, "How Core Beliefs Shape Our Perspective and Behaviour," *Psychologs*, accessed January 17, 2026, charlesmastroni.com/corebeliefs.

- what is true [knowledge].

- what is right or wrong [ethics].

- how something affects our eternal fate [salvation].

For example, a person with low self-worth will continue to repeat the patterns of negative self-talk, which affects their brain chemistry. This starts with a belief that turns into a reality for that person. Unless their idea of themself (their anthropology) changes to something positive, they will repeat these defeatist actions in their life.

Patterns of positive beliefs also have the same effect. A person who is confident they have a good sense of humor will enjoy making others laugh and will find levity in people and situations. This leads to a more enjoyable life, which will affect the person's brain chemistry, demeanor and even facial expressions. When someone performs well physically, their body releases endorphins, which create feelings of pleasure that reinforce that activity. If they also believe they're a decent athlete, this positive experience can strengthen patterns in the brain that boost confidence and motivation.

By contrast, a person with a gambling addiction gets a rush of dopamine from the risk associated with betting, which sets powerful reinforcement patterns in the brain. Since we are an integrated whole consisting of our individual mind, body and spirit, one affects the other inseparably.

It is no surprise that medicines can help the spiritual self when it becomes trapped in harmful patterns of attention deficit hyperactivity disorder (ADHD), anxiety, depression or bipolar disorder. These medicinal treatments can free the stuck brain pattern and give the person a new perspective leading to a changed belief and an improved life. However, for this to work, the changed individual must believe the new truth that they need medicine and that the improved life is good, true and real.

An extreme example of the physical brain controlling a person is addiction. Once someone is addicted to anything, control shifts from the individual's choices to feeding the fix, whether it is an addiction to a substance, like drugs or alcohol, or a behavior, like gambling or kleptomania. The common term *fix* describes the release of dopamine and other triggers in the brain's pleasure centers, where the addiction crowds out all other sources of pleasure and completely controls the individual self, even if the person knows better and wants otherwise.

A less dramatic but no less controlling brain pattern is present in a person who has to have the approval of others and cannot say no. This desire to be a people-pleaser is often subconscious, yet it controls a person's life even when they are stretched beyond their limits of time and energy.[8] Even if they want to break the pattern, they cannot do it without experiencing intense stress, because the controlling desire causes the individual to believe they need the approval of others more than anything else. These examples make it clear that physical brain patterns can and do end up controlling our individual selves.

People have subconscious, yet controlling, patterns of beliefs. If those patterns are negative, they can produce workaholics, thrill seekers, or those who want to be the center of attention. It also results in those who are constantly angry, fearful, shy, vain, domineering, pushy, overly competitive, or are dealing with a poor or inflated self-esteem. Yet we all have our patterns of thoughts. Therefore, any changes we make must come from a different set of beliefs than our current ones. Our minds are altered when we discover new truths that are then reinforced by behavior. Once ingrained, these truths can produce altered patterns of thoughts and feelings, which result in changes in ourselves. True and good beliefs lead to positive changes, and false or harmful beliefs lead to negative ones.

---

[8] Cathy Caballero, "Can't say no? Why sometimes it's fine to decline," Deakin University, accessed January 8, 2026, charlesmastroni.com/sayno.

Some people are born with genetic propensities for addictions, mental health issues, and other hindrances to the brain's proper functioning. These genetic predispositions also shape a person's beliefs, choices and actions in response to the world. This leads to an interesting question: What is a person responsible for? The answer is twofold, but to get to it, you must decide: First, does a person have control over their beliefs, decisions and actions? And second, does a person's belief patterns control the individual so they have no choice at all?

To shorten this examination, we will focus on matters of self-control that harm a person and those around them. Can an individual resist certain behaviors, or are they unable to, due to extreme chemical imbalances in their brains or deeply ingrained patterns of behavior?

A person with genetic physical defects and chemical imbalances, such as a family history of dementia, bipolar disorder or panic attacks, loses control because their brain chemistry and neuropathways actually control their actions, not the individual self. People who have these conditions do not want them, but they cannot control themselves by their will alone. An individual with severe dementia has lost control of their attention, memory and other cognitive functions because their brain no longer works properly. Someone with paranoid schizophrenia cannot help believing the world is against them, and they interpret everything from that unquestioned reality.

Change is not possible without rebalancing the brain's functioning. This differs from a person with a skeptical nature. Someone with genetic, chemical or physical abnormalities of the brain may not be able to change when they learn new information because they interpret everything through the filter of their condition. However, a skeptic can still be persuaded by new knowledge that contradicts their initial perception.

Addiction is different when it comes to self-control. Yes, it physically influences brain activity, yet the person still has a remnant of choice. An addict can change if the individual accepts the truth (namely, that they are an addict and are harming themselves and others). People can regain control and overcome drug, gambling, sex and other types of addictions when they are convinced of the truth of their condition, even if they previously denied it. However, a change in belief is essential. It leads to altered decisions and behaviors. Therapies and support groups exist to help an addict overcome addiction, but the real victory comes when they truly believe they have a problem and that indulging in the addiction even one more time would be highly dangerous.

Medicines can help stabilize brain chemistry, but overcoming an addiction requires a change in the core self of an addict. They must know and believe they have a serious problem and choose a different life. This redefines their anthropology (namely, who and what they are supposed to be as a human being). This change occurs in the core of the invisible self—the spiritual self—not the physical self, because the body is in control of addiction. Addicts often want to quit. They know and even believe what they are doing is wrong and harmful, but indulging the addiction has a hold on them through an established pattern of rushes that come from getting a fix. These are the physical payoffs for surrendering to temptation, and they control the mind, body and spirit.

Successful addiction treatment programs typically appeal to a higher power that wants the best for the individual. They draw strength from this idea that enables them to accept they are an addict and need to change.

What Christianity calls sin often acts like addiction. The apostle Paul says to the Romans:

> So I find it to be a law that when I want to do right, evil lies close at hand. For I delight in the law of God, in my inner being, but I see in my members another law waging war against the law of my mind and making me captive to the law of sin that dwells in my members. Wretched man

> that I am! Who will deliver me from this body of
> death? Thanks be to God through Jesus Christ our
> Lord! (Romans 7:21–25)

Paul is describing the conflict between his inner being, which is his core self, like his conscience, and the desires of the patterns of his mind and body that want what they want. His inner being yearns to obey God's law, while the patterns of his mind and body have no regard for it. This describes our harmful subconscious beliefs that are always with us and go unchallenged. They often win and exert control over our decisions and behaviors, just like an addict. Paul calls these "the body of sin" (Romans 6:6) because of the physical and ingrained nature of our beliefs.

Regarding personal responsibility, an individual can decide to change criminal behavior if they so choose. Criminals often know that what they are doing is wrong and harmful, but they do it anyway. Most of them decide to rape, murder and steal because they justify their desire more than wanting to do what is right. Someone engaged in criminal behavior thinks of themselves and what they want with little or no regard for their victims. Unfortunately, these cravings can take over a person's life, since they believe they have no other choice. They may even convince themselves they need to indulge these desires. What they want is their highest priority, above any ethics or value for their victims. This is a very unhealthy anthropology regarding one's fellow humans, and healthy civilizations enforce laws that prohibit such behavior.

In general, most people control their unacceptable behavior (for example, selfishness, quick temperedness, greediness or over-aggressiveness). However, we can see the resistance to new patterns of beliefs and behaviors even in less-than-sinful faults. For example, take dieting and exercise. We know when we need to lose weight, but do we? How often have you or I started a new diet with the best intentions, only to give in to old desires and patterns of behavior? The pleasure we get from certain foods makes our decision for us. We are largely unaware of this subconscious sabotage of our intentions. The same can be said of our decision to exercise. Our bodies have patterns of behavior, like minds of their own, that undercut our intentions and the accurate belief that we need to exercise for our health.

As an aside, some people are successful with diet and exercise (for example, trainers), and they say to listen to your body. But their body must be telling them something different from what my body tells me, and God bless them. If I listened to my body, I would have pancakes and bacon for breakfast, a full-sized meatball sub for lunch with a milkshake, steak or pasta for every supper, and snacks in between meals. And I would weigh well over three hundred pounds. Kidding aside, people who are successful with new diet and exercise programs instill healthier patterns of behavior based on true beliefs. As a result, they *can* overcome persistent harmful beliefs and habits.

What is the key factor in changing harmful behaviors? The person must adopt a new belief. A reformed criminal has changed their mind to value the rights of others over their own wants and desires. When a person with bipolar disorder feels more stable, they often believe they no longer need their medicine. However, the disorder soon takes hold of them again. By recognizing their need for their medication, they regain self-control as they resume taking it.

In all these cases, the change of belief occurs in the individual's invisible spiritual self, the core self that we rarely question. Harmful behavior originates with damaging beliefs in the inner self. Human decisions are ultimately the result of core truths that shape a person's worldview and life patterns. As I stated before, what we hold to be true actually molds our individual selves, our lives and, by extension, society at large. These beliefs actually become part of our identity. Remember, the mind, body and spirit are all connected. This is why we should believe what is true, good and real instead of whatever we feel like believing. Taking actual truths into our minds and hearts is like taking nourishing food into our bodies—the truth makes us healthy and strong. As Jesus taught, "You will know the truth, and the truth will set you free" (John 8:32).

Of course, beliefs are deeply personal, even the harmful ones, and when challenged, we take offense. Telling a pushy person they are pushy will probably lead to an argument. Telling a micromanaging boss they are micromanaging will not go well. How do you and I react when we are confronted with unpleasant facts about ourselves? When we disagree about what is true, we feel attacked because our beliefs are part of us. You may have had this response to some of what I have written here. And if you were to challenge me on some of my beliefs, I would react the same way.

To emphasize an important point, strong desires can be deceptive—larger truths are ignored and lies are believed, while facts are disregarded or deflected. A classic example of this is romantic love. When someone strongly loves another, they refuse to acknowledge or see the faults of the other person. We see this in the common expression "love is blind." Some people want love or companionship so badly, they ignore serious faults in the object of their affections that are obvious to others. This can happen to anyone, including people we consider to be mature and otherwise well-adjusted.

On a more troubling level, we see this in the phenomenon of catfishing, when con artists exploit someone's desire for love to scam them out of their money. People give thousands of dollars to complete strangers. These people are not crazy or stupid. They simply have a powerful desire to be loved and believe the scammer's lying story and image. The desire is so strong that they ignore the obvious truth and clear warning signals.

When it comes to God, people also have strong desires that create their beliefs. Some resist any notion of him, while others embrace him wholeheartedly. In either case, we intuitively know, if God exists, and I believe he does, we must acknowledge him, which will lead to a change in oneself.

Let's take another look at the question from the beginning of this chapter: "Why can't I believe whatever I want?"

Unfortunately, you can. But is that healthy or wise? True beliefs lead to a healthy life individually and in our cultures, while false and harmful beliefs lead to a destructive life for ourselves and our society. I want the best for you, dear reader, and I assume you want that for yourself too.

Impact of Beliefs

Let's recap here. What a person believes will largely determine who and what they are, what they do, and how they live. Beliefs become part of the individual. The self or spirit inside our bodies is invisible, along with our thoughts, emotions and will. As the inner self uses our body's senses, intellect and instincts, we learn and believe as we grow. The results are stored in our brains, nervous systems, and muscles.

We are taught ideas and come to accept them as valid or not. They may be true, false or even partially true. However, what we believe becomes part of our inner self and guides us throughout life. When we encounter new experiences and ideas, we measure them against our current beliefs and interpret life through them. We grow up in a family, a nation, and a culture that influence all these while also shaping our identity. We hone an instinct or inner sense that measures truth and falsehood as well as right and wrong. Yes, this is a very basic synopsis of human development. However, it summarizes how we experience life, and our internal health fully depends on what we believe to be true and real. This is how deeply our beliefs about theology, anthropology, knowledge, morals and the afterlife affect us.

You can see how believing a lie can damage a person. What is the truth? What is good? What is right? The answers to these questions are all a result of our worldview as outlined by the TAKES model. This is why belief in God is so important.

Let's look at some of the differences in the beliefs of an adult raised with the truth of God versus one raised with those of science and philosophy. When secular beliefs are passed on to us as truth, they inevitably shape our conclusions, like a thought train rolling down the rails with very few sidetracks. Then, eventually, these become our identities. This is an intentionally stark contrast between the answers to the questions of who and what we humans are, and what our belief systems are.

- Does God exist?
  - **Secular**: There is no God, or we are not sure if there is one. According to science, everything that exists happened by chance, including life itself. All people evolved from apes originally and are created by their parents having sex. This is taught in most Western schools, in fact. You are a combination of genes that determine who and what you are; they make you, you. However, your life is primarily determined by your abilities, which are defined by your genetic and chemical makeup and the environment you were raised in.
  - **Christian**: God, the Creator of the entire universe, thought it was a good idea to make you, even before time began. This is where your worth comes from. You are a special and unique individual. There never was, and never will be, another you. You have a will, a mind that can learn, and a spirit that can know your Creator and recognize truth. You have God-given talents and abilities. God can guide your life, and with his help and your determination, you can overcome almost any obstacle. You have an eternal soul that can go to heaven and live in his kingdom after life here ends.

- What is humankind?
  - **Secular**: You have abilities as a result of your genetic makeup. Unfortunately, you are going to have to compete with others with similar talents and skills, and your success depends on how well you do. If you want to, you may also choose to serve society to make the world a better place. (The meaning of the word *better* depends on your personal definition, based on the societal values you hold to be true.) Physically, even if your genes say you are male or female, many people believe gender is not binary. It may feel as though you have the wrong body, regardless of your genes, so if you want to become the opposite gender, you can alter your body to fit your feelings. Medical science will help you do that.
  - **Christian**: Your mom and dad consider you a gift from God. You have a special place in the history of life on the planet and a unique purpose from your Creator. He has given you gifts and talents to use because he wants you to love and serve him and others. With this foundation, you will live a meaningful life and make the world a better place by God's standards.
- Where does knowledge come from?
  - **Secular**: We don't really know what our purpose is because the universe and life are random. Governments make their own rules, and we have to follow them or be punished. Society generally believes these rules, but they can change over time. If you want a good life, you'd better prepare yourself and sharpen your abilities because competition is tough out there. Survival of the fittest is what counts, and that means being smarter, more talented, and stronger than others. This is especially true if you want to marry and have children or

have them out of wedlock. And regarding knowledge, we are on the same level as animals—just one species among many with no special place in nature. We can learn morals from the animal kingdom.

- o **Christian**: You have value because, like every person, you were made in the image of God. Therefore, you should treat others fairly and follow his rules. You are in a privileged place in his creation, having been given dominion over all the earth, to discover and learn all about the world God made for people to live in and take care of.

- What is right and wrong?

- o **Secular**: You must win. You are responsible for complying with what society will accept and what the government and culture claim is right. Otherwise, you might be fined, imprisoned or sentenced to death (or, in evolutionary terms, permanently removed from the gene pool).

- o **Christian**: We are all responsible to God to live according to what he declares is right and true. He commands that we love our neighbor and live by the Golden Rule of treating others the way we want to be treated. He knows what is best. His love, wisdom and goodness are behind the creation of the world, and his rules for living are for our benefit.

- Is there life after death?

- o **Secular**: While you may have a soul that lives on after death, science has not confirmed this. There might be a god and an afterlife, but we are not sure. What we really know from science is that you are a physical human being made of genes and chemical reactions. You may simply cease to exist when you die! But many believe in concepts like karma or reincarnation that would inform the way we live in this world. Therefore, live as best as you can to fit into society and be accepted by people, and do whatever you need to do to be successful on your own terms. If you don't believe there is any accountability for how you live, then do whatever pleases you that you can get away with. Express yourself, indulge yourself in whatever makes you feel good. To hell with society's norms and rules. If it feels good, do it!

o **Christian**: You have a soul that lives forever. God will make a perfect world, an afterlife, for those who trust, believe and obey him. If God calls to you and you accept his salvation in Christ, he will revive and perfect the image of God that he made you to be. He will guide you to live right. We can be with him eternally in his perfect heaven.

When we consider the scientific theories and post-Christian philosophies commonly taught in Western schools, the resulting worldview is bleak and depressing. From this perspective, science reduces life to complete determinism: you are powerless to rise above your genetic makeup. Your will, choices and efforts cannot fundamentally change you into anything more than what your genes permit. No matter how hard you try, you are no better than an animal in that regard.

Science offers no assurance that anything is left of you when you die. You may completely cease to be. If there is no afterlife, what is the purpose of living well? According to science, we end up as a pile of dust motes and random molecules, with no more you. Even if you outcompete everyone, you are still nothing at the end of your life. You have no memory, no consciousness, and no satisfaction of a life well lived.

American comedian Lily Tomlin popularized the saying, "The trouble with the rat race is that even if you win, you're still a rat."[9] What kind of life is that?

In contrast, the Christian worldview is full of hope and possibility because the image of God is within us, along with the promise of eternity in his perfect kingdom. This gives us a reason to strive to be the best we can be. We value doing what is good and true because we have a soul that endures, and we will live forever with the consequences of how we acted in this life. We also have a will and the ability to change and improve ourselves and the world around us. This matters not only for us but also for those we love, who will likewise live eternally—and with the impact of how we treated them and how they lived. Our lives matter because we are not merely animals with a predetermined fate. The image of God resides within us, and we have the free will to choose whether to live in light of it.

In the five questions above, drawn from the TAKES model, I intentionally drew a sharp contrast because what we were taught when our minds and beliefs were forming directs us toward truth or bends us toward falsehoods. What do you think and believe to be true?

Jesus says in Matthew 6:23, "If then the light in you is darkness, how great is the darkness!" If your guiding light is not truth and your set of beliefs is darkness, "then how great is the darkness?"

God is plainly seen in creation, and he calls to us in our hearts and through nature. He can reshape you if you believe in him and trust him to. God will show you his love, your worth to him, and your purpose, giving you meaning, peace of mind, and eternal life.

On a deep personal level, our minds need the truth. Truth equals reality. Objective truth is something that is consistently

---

[9] The original source of this quote is not clear although Lily Tomlin is often credited with making it popular. "Quote Origin: Even If You Win the Rat Race, You're Still a Rat," Quote Investigator, September 28, 2014, charlesmastroni.com/ratrace.

true without distortion by personal feelings, prejudices or interpretations. Holding false beliefs (or believing in relative truth based on your own interpretation) results in living in unreality. God is real, and he is the source of creation. As we will show in "The Origin of Creation" (starting on page 60), if you exist, then objective truth and reality must as well since nothing can be without them. False beliefs distort the mind, for lies are typically twisted forms of truth.

Socrates was right when he said, "An unexamined life is not worth living." So what do you believe? And is it the truth?

CHAPTER 3

Prevalent False Beliefs

It's my understanding that in the present culture, truth and morality are considered relative. And nothing could be further from reality. Another false belief is that all religions are the same. These misconceptions distort our perception and keep us from knowing and experiencing God. Let's take a closer look at them.

Truth and Morality Are Relative

Many people believe that reality and truth are purely relative—that nothing can be stated as universally or absolutely true. Yet such claims collapse under their own weight, since declaring "All truth is relative" is itself an attempt to make an absolute statement.[10]

Truth is not relative. For example, you exist whether or not anyone else thinks so. You are alive, and that is not debatable. This book exists; you are reading it. Nothing is relative about that. Life and death exist as well. They are objective realities. Human beings give birth to other humans, animals to animals of their species, and plants do the same. The Earth rotates around the sun and spins on its axis, which causes day and night. Gravity keeps objects from

---

[10] Clarence L. Haynes Jr., "What Is the Difference Between Absolute Truth and Relative Truth?," *Christianity.com*, May 3, 2022, charlesmastroni.com/truth.

flying into space. Newtonian laws of physics are objectively true on this planet, which happens to be where we all live. Weightlessness in outer space does not make gravity false. It still works on the Earth. The idea that all truth is relative allows for your truth versus another's. We need objectivity so we have a common ground for relating to each other.

Let's look at an example of a common situation. We can easily see the lie of relative truth in court cases where one person loans money to another and later sues for lack of repayment. The borrower may often claim, "I don't feel like I owe them anything because…" This is their "truth," shaped by the fact they didn't repay the loan and don't want to. Yet if the money was indeed a loan, the debt is an objective reality—they owe it and must repay it. When they refuse, they manufacture their truth to excuse their actions and deny the debt. That's lying, and it starts with self-deception.

You see, the easiest person to deceive is yourself. When we want or don't want something to be true, we try to justify ourselves and convince others to believe our lie. The only relativity in this situation is what the borrower and the judge choose to believe. They may accept the objective truth or not. The lender knows what is real; the recipient clings to their lie. As long as the evidence is strong enough, the judge will rule in favor of what is right and just.

The objective truth is simple: a loan was made and it needs to be repaid. Justice is served when reality is acknowledged and acted upon. Relativity enters only in the mind's ability to accept or reject the objective truth. In our example, the loan happened. All events that have ever happened are real and true. They are written into the fabric of time. The human mind may see them as they are or from its own unique perspective, which can be incomplete and biased.

This is clear in the case of an automobile accident. There is an objective reason for the event. However, the participants and witnesses will state their relative truth about what happened and why, but their accounts may be limited due to their perspective at the time.

Many people claim science is objective, but morality is relative. But is murder always wrong? What about child molestation, stealing, sex trafficking, or rape? If you answer yes to any of these, you already acknowledge that some morality is objective.[11] If you answer no, by definition, you are amoral. Nearly every civilized society has laws against these crimes because they are objectively wrong. When sociological or psychological circumstances, such as poverty or mental illness, are used to excuse immoral acts, it introduces moral relativism and undermines individual responsibility and moral agency.

It is a lie to claim moral relativity for criminals simply because they have lived a hard life. Even thieves don't want their possessions stolen. Perhaps the spouse abuser witnessed or experienced physical abuse growing up—but does that justify abusing their own spouse or children? *No.* That is why abusers can apologize convincingly: deep down, they know it's wrong. Maybe a child molester was molested as a child—but does that excuse them defiling others? *No.* Sexual abuse of anyone is still objectively wrong.

Recognizing that personal pain can contribute to criminal behavior may help with prevention or rehabilitation, but it does not change the objective morality of such acts. Civilized societies cannot excuse crime without punishing or stopping it, for to do so under the guise of relative morality is to justify it. Certain behaviors are objectively wrong and must be confronted, or civilization will break down.

The statement that all truth is relative is like someone saying, "Let me tell you the absolute truth: everything I say is a lie." If everything they say is a lie, then they can't tell the truth. And if their statement about truth being relative is true, then it's not actually true because everything they say is a lie. It's a mental treadmill.

Returning to our earlier loan example, even if the borrower genuinely feels they don't owe the money, the fact remains that

---

[11] Tim Keller, *The Reason for God: Belief in an Age of Skepticism* (New York: Penguin Books, 2009).

they must repay it if it was indeed a loan. Strong feelings or desires do not change objective truth or morality. A child molester has an overwhelming sexual desire for children, but that doesn't change the objective morality that molestation is wrong and such desires must not be acted upon.

To claim there is no objective truth or morality—and that all truth or morality is relative—is one of the worst lies because it leads to the conclusion that nothing is truly right, and consequently, nothing is wrong. Relativism has the same effect on truth: nothing can be true or false since people have different opinions. For a civilization to remain healthy over the long term, both its people and its government must reject what is wrong.

Relativism claims that morality is based on cultural norms. While it's true cultures differ in certain moral practices, this does not mean there is no objective morality. Nor does it explain where cultural norms come from in the first place or diminish the fact that most contain a substantial amount of objective morality. Moral relativism holds that all knowledge, truth, morals and beliefs exist within a framework of some kind—whether it is a larger culture, a religion, a scientific community, a school of psychology or philosophy, a political group, or some other organization.

Moral relativism does not account for the ultimate source of these frameworks. As we discussed in Chapter 2, morals come from outside the human mind. At some point in history, people recognized objective truth and what is morally right to the best of their understanding. They may have been the great moral teachers who founded many of the religions that have shaped our cultures over the centuries. They communicated these truths and moral principles, but did not invent them.

The universe cannot exist without objective truth because then nothing could be real. The Creator of the universe is also the Creator of ultimate truth and morality. God is the source of reality, the cause of all things. The universe is designed to function according to objective principles, which science seeks to uncover. In the same way, humanity is designed to live and act in alignment with moral truths. Great thinkers and religious founders have recognized this fact throughout history. Objective truth and morality have always existed because the Creator intended us to live by them. Once they were discovered, they could be internalized and passed down from generation to generation, eventually forming the foundation of cultural norms.

Our Creator also placed within each of us some knowledge of good and evil in the form of our individual conscience. This enables humanity to recognize and live within the framework of objective morality. Civilizations that attempted to weave this morality into their cultural fabric were able to grow, while those that abandoned it ultimately destroyed themselves.

Objective truth and morality exist outside the human mind, having been created by the designer of the universe. Without them, there can be no truth or morality at all. However, the notion of relativity comes from the limitations of the human will to grasp these concepts and a resistance to accept them.

Let's look at how morality becomes incorporated into an individual. We already established earlier that children are born with little understanding of right and wrong. They simply want what they need and desire, as the terrible twos and threes show us. A child first learns much of morality from their parents, then from interactions with others. This socialization process is largely shaped by cultural norms. Ultimately, the moral framework of their environment shapes their mind. It exists outside the individual, who learns right from wrong according to the values of their family, which is in turn influenced by their culture. That framework may align closely with, or deviate from, the Creator's objective moral framework.

In the Bible, God's love for humanity is likened to a father's love for his children. We are not equal to God, nor is our human love the same as his. God is the perfect Father and is the source of objective morality. His love perfects us and moves us to conform to his moral standards.

Just as a child does not become a productive adult without proper parental discipline and instruction, we are not transformed into the image of God without his correction. Yet what is healthy discipline? The root of the word *discipline* is the same as the root for *disciple*. Both words come from the Latin *discipulus*, which means "pupil" or "learner."[12] When God disciplines you or me, it is so we learn to follow his ways. (Discipline is not only punishment. It can also refer to training, as when a coach trains an athlete in their sport.)

Morality varies from family to family and from culture to culture. What a child sees, experiences and learns early in life profoundly shapes them. An extreme example would be of a child raised in a loving home that practices respect, fairness and kindness versus that same child being raised in an abusive home. The values and morals learned in childhood typically produce very different outcomes in adulthood. Yet some individuals defy a healthy upbringing by becoming amoral, while others overcome an amoral upbringing to become highly moral. Thus, the external framework for morality is not a guarantee of how an individual will turn out, but it is a major factor. Another significant influence is a well-formed conscience. Is it grounded in objective morality or clouded by personal justifications?

Cultural morality is typically reflected in laws and norms, both explicit and implicit, and shapes the expectations for individual behavior. No culture is uniformly good and moral, and no family is perfect either. For the purposes of this book, we can reasonably say that for a civilization or society to endure and prosper over long periods, it must uphold a moral framework that fosters stability, cooperation and trust among its people. History has shown, time and again, that when a community deviates from such morality, it fails. Such frameworks, while far from perfect, have generally included values that accommodate productivity, creativity and intellectual growth. Again, no culture or governmental system,

---

[12] *Merriam-Webster Dictionary*, "discipline," accessed January 8, 2026, charles-mastroni.com/discipline.

from kings to democracies, is perfect, but history shows that a moral framework with values that are broadly beneficial and just is essential for long-term survival and flourishing.

Let's revisit where the truth and moral framework of a culture come from: historically, they have grown out of the great religions and philosophies. These frameworks existed before the individual learned them. How did the great religious leaders and philosophers acquire them? They were drawn by truth itself to seek what is objectively right and moral. Remember, such realizations are discovered, not invented. These leaders often describe their experiences as inspired and say they had a revelation, vision or moment of profound insight. They find what they find, discover what they discover, and then communicate these ideas—offering beneficial knowledge that has shaped and influenced various cultures throughout the world.

The inspiration comes from outside themselves. The only one with objective truth and morality is the Maker of all things—God. Even the greatest human minds are enlightened by an all-knowing Creator. He is the author of objective truth and morality because he is the source of knowledge and wisdom.

The existence of the frameworks of truth and morals has the same source as that of the physical universe. Since matter and energy change, they do not possess the power of existence within themselves. The same applies to morality and truth in the minds of humanity. Perfect, objective morality exists outside us—in eternity. These frameworks share the same ultimate cause and foundation as the physical universe: the God who is, who was, and who will always be—the eternal God.

In Plato's allegory of the cave, the people within the cave only see shadows of objects projected on the walls, yet believe what they are viewing is reality. Plato was illustrating that ultimate reality—and the purest forms of truth, knowledge, beliefs and morals—exists beyond the world we perceive, while what we see here are merely shadows of those higher realities. The images before us are relative imitations of objective truth and morality. Perfection and permanence reside elsewhere. What we experience in life are reflections of the frameworks of truth and morals. Plato may not have had all the right answers, but his allegory affirmed that the perfection of real things lies beyond the human mind and the visible, physical world. Perfection lies in eternity, not time.

Truth equals reality. Since there is an objective reality, there is also objective truth. As we established earlier, our beliefs are what we hold to be valid or not. They can align more closely—or drift further away—from objective truth and reality. In this way, our beliefs fall along a continuum, ranging from accurate to distorted. While no human is perfect, God is. He alone possesses a perfect will, an objective existence, ultimate truth, and infinite goodness. Without God's holiness (his absolute pure love and incorruptibility), the universe would deteriorate into corruption, disorder and decay. He gave humanity a large degree of freedom to live in accordance with objective morality or to reject it, which is why we see both good and evil in this world.

Again, the apostle Paul in Romans addresses the question of belief this way:

> For what can be known about God is plain to [people], because God has shown it to them. For his invisible attributes, namely, his eternal power and divine nature, have been clearly perceived, ever since the creation of the world, in the things that have been made. So they are without excuse. For although they knew God, they did not honor him as God or give thanks to him, but they became futile in their thinking, and their foolish hearts were darkened. Claiming to be wise, they became fools, and exchanged the glory of the immortal God for images resembling mortal man and birds and animals and creeping things.

Therefore God gave them up in the lusts of their hearts to impurity, to the dishonoring of their bodies among themselves, because they exchanged the truth about God for a lie and worshipped and served the creature rather than the Creator, who is blessed forever! Amen (Romans 1:19–25).

A fundamental belief that is foundational to our psyche is this: "Does God exist or not?" What do you believe? How you answer this question is the cornerstone of your mind, belief and worldview.

> There is objective morality.
> Right and wrong have finality.
>
> We can make our own rules if we choose,
> but eternal blessings, we may lose.
>
> Within our conscience's sight,
> there is knowledge of wrong and right.
>
> If relative morality is your dictum,
> I suggest you ask crime victims.
>
> Your theory should be tested
> by a child who was molested.
>
> Tell a victim of spousal abuse
> they should not be so obtuse.
>
> Tell those wounded by a lie,
> they have no reason to cry.

For better or worse, God made humanity free. We can believe in him or not. We can obey him or not. But there are unavoidable consequences when our minds wander from the truth of God. What does your conscience tell you? A mind and soul steeped in false beliefs will inevitably be unable to find objective reality or morality.

Let's define true freedom. It is not a license to do whatever we want or to indulge every desire. Some practical examples include a cultural norm and law against stealing. If someone justifies theft in their own mind or if a culture permits it by law as "freedom," the way some rioters have done throughout history, would that lead to a prosperous, civilized society? No. And would the thief be truly free? No, because they themselves could be robbed at any moment. The less stealing there is in a society, the more genuine freedom its people enjoy.

The same principle applies to addiction. Is a drug user free when they take drugs, or are they enslaved by their condition? Clearly, they are trapped—as are their family and friends, those affected by their choices. Which makes society freer: restricting (and even prohibiting) drug use or legalizing it in the name of freedom?

What about no-cash bail programs that release violent offenders before trial? These people may be set loose to indulge their impulses, but does that make the rest of us freer? According to *CBS News*, violent offenders are three times more likely to be rearrested when released on no-cash bail.[13] Yet these practices have become common in many states and cities in the US. The results are not greater freedom, but greater danger for society as a whole—and an increase in the harm caused to potential victims.

For a less extreme example, what about the rules of travel? What if we were free to ignore traffic laws altogether? For example, what if airplanes could take off and land whenever they wanted, without the guidance of air traffic controllers? When everyone obeys the law, we are all free to travel wherever we wish and arrive safely. But when they are ignored, freedom quickly disappears. Accidents, traffic jams, and plane crashes multiply in proportion to the violations. The more people drive the way they want, the less freedom we all have to reach our destinations. Actual freedom depends on fair laws and the obedience of society's members.

---

[13] Julie Watts, "Updated $0 bail study: Suspects released had twice felony rearrests, three times the violent crime rearrests," *CBS News*, updated January 17, 2025, charlesmastroni.com/zerobail.

The same is true with God. His rules and laws for living grant us freedom, while disobeying them ultimately destroys it.

If you decide to use a car as a boat, it will not work. You may be free to do so, but you risk drowning. If you try to use an airplane as a car, you won't get very far in your journey through life. But when cars, planes and boats are used as they were designed, they work well. It is the same with people. Real freedom and fulfillment come when we live as we were created to, within God's rules.

However, much of today's culture thinks freedom means "anything goes"—that whatever people want to do should be allowed, no matter what. For instance, some argue that the use of hard drugs (heroin, opioids, etc.) should be permitted for adults because they are only hurting themselves, not anyone else.[14] But is that really true? Drug use often leads to lost jobs, stealing from others, abandoning family obligations, and an avoidable drain on medical resources. In many cases, it also leads to assaults and even murder, all to support the habit. Legalizing hard drugs will not eliminate the negative consequences for the addicts themselves or for those they harm. Therefore, permitting the use of drugs is not true freedom. If an addict wants treatment and support to get and stay clean, that should be encouraged and provided. However, passing laws to make hard drug use legal is a mistaken idea of freedom.

Another example people often give of "freedom" is the idea that two consenting adults can do whatever they want sexually. But does this supposed freedom truly harm no one? What if one or both of them are married? Spouses and families are deeply affected by infidelity, which is why it has long been recognized as grounds for divorce. Even if neither person is married, casual sex often leaves behind emotional pain, broken trust, and in some cases sexually

---

14 Alexis S. Hammond, Kelly E. Dunn, and Eric C. Strain, "Drug Legalization and Decriminalization Beliefs Among Substance-using and Nonusing Individuals," *Journal of Addiction Medicine* 14, no. 1 (Jan.–Feb. 2020): 56–62, accessed January 8, 2026, doi.org/10.1097/ADM.0000000000000542.

transmitted diseases or children born without a stable home life. These consequences extend far beyond the individuals involved.

A more extreme example of this is an adult choosing to have sex with children. To make this seem more acceptable, they describe this condition with neutral language and refer to themselves as being a "minor-attracted person," but that's only to reduce the stigma and separate attraction from criminal acts. Pedophilia and sex trafficking are rampant internationally, and child pornography offenses in the US alone increased 34.4 percent between 2020 and 2024.[15] Should people be free to indulge? Does the progressive definition of freedom apply to these behaviors?

What may look like freedom on the surface often produces ripple effects of hurt, instability and loss for others. True freedom does not mean indulging every desire. It means living within God's design in a way that builds up rather than tears down. The popular phrase "with great power comes great responsibility" is true. Freedom is the power to choose. Therefore, if we want to be free, there must be accountability for our choices.

What are the rules of morality that will provide true freedom? The Bible is called the "written Word of God," and it expresses his will for humanity, including the Ten Commandments and God's plan for the sacrament of marriage, among others.

Jesus teaches that God's law is still valid and should be fulfilled. In the gospel of Matthew, Jesus says:

> Do not think that I have come to abolish the Law or the Prophets; I have not come to abolish them but to fulfill them. For truly, I say to you, until heaven and earth pass away, not an iota, not a dot, will pass from the Law until all is accomplished (Matthew 5:17–18).

---

[15] United States Sentencing Commission, *FY24 Quick Facts on Child Pornography Offenses*, Fiscal Year 2024 (Washington, DC: US Sentencing Commission, 2025), charlesmastroni.com/childstats.

Using the TAKES model, this accounts for Jesus's teaching on ethics as it relates to salvation.

Does true love and freedom mean we condone all behavior and desires as acceptable just to make people feel good about themselves? A good parent sets rules and expects obedience from their children so they learn right from wrong. In the same way, God has set rules for living and expects obedience to them, rules based on his wisdom and design, and communicated in the Ten Commandments (Exodus 20:1–17, condensed):

1. I am the Lord your God. You shall have no other gods before me.
2. You shall not make idols.
3. You shall not take the name of the Lord your God in vain.
4. Remember the Sabbath day, to keep it holy.
5. Honor your father and your mother.
6. You shall not murder.
7. You shall not commit adultery.
8. You shall not steal.
9. You shall not bear false witness against your neighbor.
10. You shall not covet. (In other words, you shall not desire the goods or spouse of others.)

Jesus also shared what is commonly referred to as the Golden Rule: "So in everything, do to others what you would have them do to you, for this sums up the Law and the Prophets" (Matthew 7:12 NIV). This is true love and freedom.

But does that mean we need to accept all behavior and desires simply to please people? This is a cheap imitation of love and lacks wisdom. Taking this approach would be like a parent who indulges every demand of their children. These kids rarely turn out well.

True love includes truth, wisdom and concern for the well-being of others.

Some human desires and behaviors are wrong, and even evil. They can also significantly harm others. Such impulses should not be indulged since the behavior of spoiled adults typically drives others away, resulting in a lonely life because they are intolerable to be around. If evil behavior is unchecked, offenders may indulge in criminal desires that will end in rejection by society (in the form of prison or ostracism). No amount of policing will maintain civilized life if too many people don't adhere to God's law.

Genuine love and freedom must include protection from evil or harmful desires, and caring for someone means correcting them when they are doing wrong. A healthy response to the love of a good parent is to learn from and obey them and incorporate those lessons into your heart. This leads to living a productive life and enjoying greater freedom.

On a community level, a healthy response to God's love is learning, obeying and incorporating his teaching into our lives. When we depart from this, we end up in trouble. That is not true freedom.

A judgment day is coming for every one of us, and there is no deceiving God. He will allow us the liberty and the foolishness to deceive ourselves. But lies and false ideas of freedom cannot stand on judgment day, which Jesus himself is recorded in the Bible as clearly stating will come.

> Just as the weeds are gathered and burned with fire, so will it be at the end of the age. The Son of Man [Jesus] will send his angels, and they will gather out of his kingdom all causes of sin and all law-breakers, and throw them into the fiery furnace. In that place there will be weeping and gnashing of teeth. Then the righteous will shine like the sun in the kingdom of their Father. He who has ears, let him hear (Matthew 13:40–43, words added).

You may want to believe there is no such thing as judgment day because you don't like the idea of it, but that doesn't mean this belief is true. Our likes and dislikes do not create reality. God does.

All Religions Are the Same

Many statements are accepted as true or truisms in our current culture that are not. One is the common platitude that all religions are the same. Despite the clear differences between them, many people still hold this view without ever investigating for themselves. Each religion has its own belief system, and they should not be mixed and matched. What you hold to be true creates the world you live in. Without the solid foundation of a trustworthy religion, adopting various beliefs will create confusion.

Admittedly, I am not an expert on all religions, but we can easily observe they are different. Some religions have one God, while others have many gods. Still others are based on a philosophy of what life should be about. Most religions with multiple gods attach deities to powerful natural phenomena, resulting in the worship of the sun, moon and gods in charge of fertility, love, health, oceans, Hades, the sky, crop growth, rain, lightning, winds, rivers and others. The apostle Paul describes these religions in Romans 1:25. "They exchanged the truth about God for a lie, and worshipped and served created things rather than the Creator—who is forever praised. Amen" (NIV). Basically, most polytheistic religions worship nature. Many stories in these religions cover creation, the nature of the gods and humanity, the purpose of life, fundamental truths, and a moral code, and these explanations don't agree from one tradition to the next. They also offer different worldviews of theology, anthropology, truth, ethics, salvation and the afterlife.

Other religions are based on philosophies such as Buddhism, Taoism and Shintoism. Like polytheistic religions, they also have conflicting worldviews. These are often based on the perceptions and thoughts of inspired individuals who effectively communicated their beliefs.

These teachings found widespread acceptance in the cultures where they originated and then spread from there. The founders and teachers of these religions recognized some aspects of truth, but not the whole truth of God. Due to their human origins, these beliefs are no different from those founded by classical, modern or post-modern philosophers. These religions contain elements of human wisdom that align, at least in part, with objective truth. They represent earnest efforts that push the mind to its limits in seeking to grasp objective truth and morality.

Classical Greek philosophy, like that of the traditions mentioned above, has profoundly shaped culture, particularly the Western worldview. Interestingly, Greek philosophy largely developed apart from the Olympian religion, yet it still offered significant teachings on theology, anthropology, knowledge, ethics and salvation.

The Christian understanding of philosophy-based religions is that they are part of God's grace, given to humanity in the form of a conscience, so people might live in a civilized manner. This is why there are similar ideas of what is right and wrong in most cultures. The founders of these philosophy-based religions were the most capable thinkers of their time. They sought truth earnestly and communicated it with such clarity and influence that their ideas have endured for centuries.

These religions and philosophies contain elements of truth, discernible through the human conscience—our innate sense of good and evil. While we do not have God's omniscience, he didn't leave us devoid of any knowledge. Conscience itself is also part of God's grace, enabling humanity to live with some measure of moral order.

If all we knew was evil, we would kill one another. This has happened throughout human history, in war after war and in corrupt societies. Even though the philosophy-based religions restrict evil, they do not eliminate it from the heart.

There are three major monotheistic religions: Christianity, Islam and Judaism. Even though these all believe in one omnipotent, all-wise, all-knowing creator God, they have a variety of takes on theology, anthropology, knowledge, ethics and salvation. There is some overlap among them, but there are contrasting doctrinal beliefs that result in conflicting worldviews. I cannot go into a detailed study of all religions or even these three in this book. However, all religions are not the same, and they do not produce the same worldview, culture or foundation for living, nor do they produce equivalent moral frameworks.

If every belief system offers a different understanding of God and morality, the question becomes which one reflects reality. For that, we need a trustworthy foundation. I believe the Bible offers just that. But to rely on it as authoritative, we must first explore whether it provides credible evidence for what it teaches.

CHAPTER 4

Evidence for the Bible

The Christian worldview is taken from the Bible, the primary written source of truth, knowledge and belief—about God, the world, humanity, good, evil and the afterlife. The Bible is authentic and remarkably unchanged since its original writing. God did not leave us in the dark without a permanent witness to the truth.

There are two parts to the Bible: the Old and New Testaments. The Old Testament consists of Hebrew texts that describe events ending approximately four hundred years before Jesus was born. It is ancient and well-documented, hand-copied and translated throughout the centuries. Part of the Old Testament includes the Law of Moses and the writings of the prophets whose messages proved true over time.

Jesus told us:

> Do not think that I have come to abolish the Law or the Prophets; I have not come to abolish them but to fulfill them. For truly, I say to you, until heaven and earth pass away, not an iota, not a dot, will pass from the Law until all is accomplished (Matthew 5:17–18).

Jesus quoted the Hebrew scriptures (the Old Testament) extensively and declared their validity. And in the same way, these scriptures predict the birth of the Messiah (Jesus) seven hundred years before his birth (Isaiah 7:14).[16]

The Old Testament is followed by the New Testament, which consists of the four Gospels, the book of Acts, the Epistles (or letters) and Revelation, all written by the disciples or close early followers of Jesus. Whereas the Old Testament covered events long before his birth, the New Testament documents his life and teachings as well as the establishment and growth of the early church, and the ultimate consummation of God's redemptive work at the end of time.

The Gospels—Matthew, Mark, Luke and John—are the primary accounts of Jesus's life, deeds and teachings with some additional events written in the book of Acts. Matthew and John were two of the twelve disciples who lived with the Messiah during his walk on earth. They wrote their gospels as eyewitnesses to what Jesus said and did. Mark, one of his followers, was taught by the apostle Peter, who also lived with Jesus and witnessed his words and deeds firsthand. Luke was a physician and a contemporary of the people in Jesus's life.

Scholars agree Mark's gospel was written first and then Matthew and Luke added their own accounts of their experiences with Christ. John wrote his gospel toward the end of his life, long after the others were in circulation during the first century, when the apostles and contemporaries of Jesus still lived. Early readers would have recognized any inaccuracies if they existed, since many of them were apostles themselves.

According to Luke's introduction to his gospel, he made a thorough investigation into all the events of Jesus's life. Luke records the Christmas story of Jesus's birth and Mary's account of how she came to bear the Son of God. He met and talked with

---

[16] Mark Driscoll, "Did the Old Testament predict Jesus coming into history?," *Real Faith*, accessed January 8, 2026, charlesmastroni.com/otprediction.

those who knew Jesus: his disciples, close followers and family. He also wrote the book of Acts, investigating the events of the early church and the lives of Jesus's disciples and close followers as they witnessed his life, death and resurrection. The virgin birth of Jesus and his resurrection present stumbling blocks for many people. While I address these topics more fully in the appendices of this book, I will touch briefly on them now simply to say, for God—the creator of life—impregnating a virgin without physical intercourse poses no challenge, nor would resurrecting someone from the dead.

The gospel of John was written after the other three gospels were already in circulation. We know he was a witness and follower of Jesus because he was one of the twelve disciples. This gospel is nonchronological since John was providing additional material not included in the other gospels and sharing his very personal knowledge and witness of Jesus Christ.

Luke frequently traveled with the apostle Paul, who wrote most of the Epistles, the letters to the earliest churches. The other epistle writers in the New Testament were Jesus's disciples, Peter and John, and his half brother James. Together, the human authors of the New Testament are legitimate eyewitnesses, investigators and recorders of what Jesus taught and did, who he spoke with, and the events in his life. They wrote as they were inspired to— bearing witness and offering true knowledge of Jesus Christ.

The final part of the New Testament is the book of Revelation, which was written by John. He composed it as a letter to the seven churches in Asia Minor to encourage and exhort believers to remain faithful amid trials and persecutions. Then, Revelation moves on to a vision of events leading to the end times, Armageddon and final judgment. Overall, the message describes the ultimate victory of God.

Let's look at the Bible's validity from the point of view of scholars who examine ancient documents. Textual criticism is the discipline of examining the authenticity and accuracy of ancient documents. This type of evaluation is applied not only to the Bible but to all texts from antiquity: *The Iliad*, *The Odyssey*, the *History of the Peloponnesian War*, Roman records, and any other written works that may have survived from earlier civilizations.

The Gospels and Epistles of the New Testament were hand-copied and preserved in codex form—that is, bound like a book—unlike the Old Testament scriptures, which were originally written on scrolls. But were the original texts changed over time or are they consistent?

Textual criticism assesses several key criteria to establish authenticity:

1. How many copies of the work have survived to be examined?

2. Are those copies consistent with each other?

3. Are the materials used consistent with those used in their respective times?

4. Do the surviving copies match each other in content, especially compared to the oldest ones?

As you will see in the next few pages, the New Testament holds up to all these criteria far better than other ancient documents.

The timeline of history is centered on Jesus's birth at AD 1, so his death and resurrection were in approximately AD 33. Paul lived from 5 BC to AD 62 (or possibly AD 67). Therefore, he lived up to thirty-four years with the original apostles, whom he knew and interacted with. Paul quotes the writings of Luke (Luke 10:7) in his epistle to his protégé Timothy,[17] which tells us Paul was familiar with

---

[17] First Timothy 5:18 states, "For the Scripture says, 'You shall not muzzle an ox when it treads out the grain,' and, 'The laborer deserves his wages.'" The first quotation is from the Old Testament. However, the second is a command from Jesus to his followers when he sent them out to preach and heal, taken directly from Luke 10:7. Paul's use of this Scripture demonstrates the gospel of Luke existed in Paul's time, definitely before AD 62–67. Therefore, the gospel of Luke existed less than thirty-four years after Jesus's death.

Luke's gospel. For that to be true, it had to have existed in Paul's lifetime, less than thirty years after Jesus's death and resurrection.

Many of the early church leaders, who studied and learned directly from the apostles, reference the Gospels in their surviving writings. Therefore, these texts existed in their lifetimes and were used in their teachings and in leading the early church.

Clement of Rome, who lived approximately AD 35–96, wrote to the church in Corinth and knew the apostle Paul, who mentions Clement in Philippians 4:3. Textual scholars F. C. Bauer and Lee McDonald demonstrate that First Clement, a letter written to the church in Corinth, references the gospels of Mark and Matthew, respectively.[18] Therefore, these two gospels existed in the latter half of the first century.

The Gospels were written because most of the apostles were old and dying, and they wanted to ensure Jesus's teachings and what they had witnessed were passed on to future generations. There is very strong evidence the four Gospels have survived intact since the first century.

This extensive quote from Matt Slick's article entitled "Manuscript evidence for superior New Testament reliability" (used with permission) provides more details regarding that:

> The New Testament is constantly under attack, and its reliability and accuracy are often contested by critics. But, there is ample manuscript evidence for superior New Testament reliability over all other ancient documents. If the critics want to disregard the New Testament, then they must also disregard other ancient writings by Plato, Aristotle and Homer. This is because the New Testament documents are better preserved and more

---

[18] Jacob J. Prahlow, "Scripture in 1 Clement: Composite Citation of the Gospels (Part I)," *Pursuing Veritas*, accessed January 8, 2026, charlesmastroni. com/1clement.

numerous than any other ancient writings. Because they are so numerous, they can be cross-checked for accuracy … and they are very consistent.

There are presently 5,686 Greek manuscripts in existence today for the New Testament. If we were to compare the number of New Testament manuscripts to other ancient writings, we find that the New Testament manuscripts far outweigh the others in quantity.

Author	Date written	Earliest copy	Approximate time span between original & copy	Number of copies	Accuracy of copies
Lucretius	died 55 or 53 BC		1,100 yrs	2	—
Pliny	AD 61–113	AD 850	750 yrs	7	—
Plato	427–347 BC	AD 900	1,200 yrs	7	—
Demosthenes	4th cent. BC	AD 1100	800 yrs	8	—
Herodotus	480–425 BC	AD 900	1,300 yrs	8	—
Suetonius	AD 75–160	AD 950	800 yrs	8	—
Thucydides	460–400 BC	AD 900	1,300 yrs	8	—
Euripides	480–406 BC	AD 1100	1,300 yrs	9	—
Aristophanes	450–385 BC	AD 900	1,200	10	—
Caesar	100–44 BC	AD 900	1,000	10	—
Livy	59 BC–AD 17	—	unknown	20	—
Tacitus	circa AD 100	AD 1100	1,000 yrs	20	—

Author	Date written	Earliest copy	Approximate time span between original & copy	Number of copies	Accuracy of copies
Aristotle	384–322 BC	AD 1100	1,400 yrs	49	—
Sophocles	496–406 BC	AD 1000	1,400 yrs	193	—
Homer (*Iliad*)	900 BC	400 BC	500 yrs	643	95%
New Testament	c. AD 50–100	2nd cent. AD (c. AD 130 f.)	less than 100 years	5600	99.5%

As you can see, there are thousands more New Testament Greek manuscripts than any other ancient writing. The internal consistency of the New Testament documents is about 99.5% textually pure. That is an amazing accuracy. In addition, there are over 19,000 copies in the Syriac, Latin, Coptic and Aramaic languages. The total supporting New Testament manuscript base is over 24,000.

Almost all biblical scholars agree that the New Testament documents were all written before the close of the First Century. If Jesus was crucified in AD 30, then that means the entire New Testament was completed within 70 years. This is important because it means there were plenty of people around when the New Testament documents were penned—people who could have contested the writings. In other words, those who wrote the documents knew that if they were inaccurate, plenty of people would have pointed it out. But, we have absolutely no ancient documents contemporary with the First Century that contest the New Testament texts.[19]

In conclusion, the Bible is authentic—a faithful witness to God's creation of the universe and humankind, and his work to save humanity. The New Testament is an accurate and reliable communication of the life, death and resurrection of Jesus Christ as well as his teachings, healings and love for humanity. Unless you insist on believing that it is made up of lies, it is an authentic account of Jesus and the salvation he offers.

God's followers wrote his word of truth:
Prophets and apostles, Old Testament and New.

God sent them his visions; they witnessed by sight.
They wrote God's story, his power, his might.

His plan to save us from the grave and from sinning.
They tell us the truth right from the beginning.

They tell us the end, what might be our fate,
Heaven or hell, God's Word stands at the gate.

---

[19] Matt Slick, "Manuscript evidence for superior New Testament reliability," CARM, December 6, 2008, charlesmastroni.com/ntreliability.

CHAPTER 5

Back to Basics

Every child asks, "Where did I come from? Where did everything come from?" This fundamental question shapes our individual psyches and worldviews. The answers form every child's belief system. You probably asked this question yourself when you were younger. The resulting belief profoundly shapes everything in the TAKES worldview that we hold to be true— our theology, anthropology, knowledge, ethics and salvation. Does God exist? What are we as human beings? What is true knowledge? Where do right and wrong come from? Is there an afterlife and, if there is, what is it like?

In this chapter, let's compare some secular, nonreligious responses with a religious answer to these questions. Since these viewpoints shape our psyche, beliefs and knowledge, it is vitally important they are true and real. All cultures attempt to resolve these fundamental childhood inquiries through their religion, philosophy, science and art. We know we exist; we know objects exist; we know life exists. The questions are always how and why, and what caused them.

The Origin of Creation

Everything is a combination of matter and energy. Matter is anything that has mass and takes up space, much of which we perceive with our senses (for example, rocks, water and air). Energy, on the other hand, has the power to cause work—it's not made of matter and doesn't take up space. Examples include light, heat and electricity. Everything that exists falls somewhere on the energy-matter continuum. Empirically, all energy and matter are in a state of change, even relatively permanent objects (for example, rocks, which are worn down over time).

While the Earth is estimated to be billions of years old, it is continually changing, as the theory of plate tectonics shows us. Supernovas are stars that explode at the end of their life cycles. All life as we know it lives and dies, comes into and out of existence. And on a much larger timescale, so do planets, suns, solar systems, galaxies and the universe. These are all bound by time and, therefore, are subject to change.

As such, these things cannot remain unchanged. Their very existence is not self-sustaining because they eventually cease to be what they were. If the cause of their being were contained within them, they would not be subject to decay. Therefore, it must lie outside of them—and outside of time. The universe, along with all matter and energy, must have been caused by someone or something beyond time that possesses the power of existence and does not depend on anything else to be.

Being is our very word for existence. For something to exist, it has to be. Therefore, whatever has the power of existence in itself is pure being and must be eternal outside time. Such an entity is the ultimate reality—the cause of all other existence—and depends on nothing else. Philosophers such as Descartes have argued existence must belong to the very essence of such a being.[20]

---

[20] "Descartes' Ontological Argument," Stanford Encyclopedia of Philosophy, updated May 5, 2025, charlesmastroni.com/descartes.

Pure being must be present for there to be any existence at all. This is a quality of God as described by classic Christian theology. He is eternal, unchanging, all-knowing, all-powerful, the Creator. God is and causes all things to come into existence because only he has the power of self-existence. In Exodus, Moses asked God what his name is so he could tell the Israelites who had sent him to save them. "God said to Moses, '*I am who I am*. This is what you are to say to the Israelites: *I am* has sent me to you'" (Exodus 3:14 NIV). God simply *is*. *He is!* And he is the cause, the Creator, of all that exists.

The secular explanation for our origin and the origin of the universe, the most prevalent view in these times, is the scientific explanation (derived from Darwin's *On the Origin of Species by Means of Natural Selection* and the Big Bang theory). Since it is so widespread and unchallenged in our secular culture, I want to consider a different perspective. Science still falls short of answering the child's question of "Where did everything come from?" Some scientists propose that all energy and matter in the universe have always existed, but as we showed above, energy and matter are not eternal or self-existing because they always change. Anything that alters over time is not eternal in nature. Therefore, it doesn't have the property of self-existence contained within itself. Nothing that exists, from the smallest to the largest, has this property or ability to be eternally what it is throughout time.

Atoms combine to form compounds that change their physical and chemical properties into something other than what they were before. According to the Big Bang theory, the universe began about 13.8 billion years ago. Everything in the observable universe was originally in a very tiny space, even smaller than an atom. A brief period of rapid expansion, precipitated by unknown energy, inflated the universe to make it the size it is today, and it has been expanding ever since. But science can offer no further explanation for the origin of the universe before time began.

If we trace back to before the Big Bang, we enter the realm of speculative physics. One hypothesis suggests that, before stable atoms or molecules were formed, the universe experienced a "grand unified epoch" during which short-lived elementary particles, such as quarks (the building blocks of protons and neutrons), were present.[21] However, our current experiments cannot generate enough energy to replicate those conditions.

Yet the immense universe exists, life exists, and you and I exist. But where did it all begin? It must start with the eternal, which is separate from time, not an extension of the passing of time. Traditional philosophers and theologians call this *creation ex nihilo,* meaning "creation from nothing." Energy and matter must come from something other than themselves that has the power of existence (namely God, who is the Creator outside creation and time). God, who has the power of existence within himself, creates from nothing by his will alone.

This is the classic Christian theology of:

> In the beginning, God created the heavens and the earth. The earth was without form and void, and darkness was over the face of the deep. And the Spirit of God was hovering over the face of the waters. And God said, "Let there be light," and there was light (Genesis 1:1–3).

The broad outline of the created universe and life itself is described in the rest of the first chapter of Genesis.

Proponents of the Big Bang theory hold that the universe was contained in an infinitely dense, ultra-small pinpoint from which it expanded into the vast cosmos we see, producing the time and space we live in, right down to this little planet perfectly and delicately balanced to support life. Now, if that doesn't sound like

---

[21] Alastair Wilson, "What existed before the Big Bang?" BBC Future, January 5, 2022, charlesmastroni.com/bigbang.

creation ex nihilo, I don't know what does. Science is essentially claiming the universe came from nothing, without admitting or accepting there is a creator, because it can't explain where any matter or energy came from before the Big Bang.

Since science doesn't know how matter or energy came to be, some researchers start with the assumption that a precursor for them existed. But this just avoids answering the question of existence, because where did this precursor come from? How did it come to be?

Then they theorize that somehow this precursor to the Big Bang became concentrated into a tiny area, and again, this sounds like creation ex nihilo. What force made pre-matter, and what kept it together? What could compress all that mass into virtually nothing? And what caused it to turn into energy and matter, then expand? Science does not answer this. Even atomic explosions pale in comparison to the vastness of the universe. And once it expanded, why didn't it contract again?

Why would it differentiate into so many types of matter and energy: stars, planets, galaxies and, eventually, life? What caused all this? Science really does not know for certain. Energy and matter are always in a state of flux. So why are there so many types of stability? Life, suns, compounds and atoms all certainly have form while they exist. Why do energy and matter take shape in the first place when they only break down over time?

The only scientific speculations, and I emphasize *speculations*, seem to be that energy and matter have an organizational property (an affinity or inclination) inherent in themselves to take forms. However, this is completely contradicted by other laws of physics, such as entropy, which states that systems tend toward the greatest degree of disorder, and ultimate entropy would be next to absolute zero, meaning no energy at all. *Merriam-Webster Dictionary* defines *entropy* as "a process of degradation or running down or a trend to disorder" and "the degradation of the matter and energy in the universe to an ultimate state of inert uniformity."[22] Yet if energy and matter naturally tend toward disorder and their lowest possible energy state, why do they have so many relatively stable forms? Stars certainly have a higher energy level than planets. Why is that? Air contains more energy than rocks. But what caused it?

When it comes to matter becoming more stable, more energetic, or more complex, these characteristics are contrary to the entropic properties of energy and matter. Why do some of their configurations form a sun and another a planet—one a gas, and another, a solid—when they both originate from an infinitely dense, uniform mass in a tiny infinitesimal spot?

There are a lot of stars and galaxies. What blueprints were they designed from? What patterns do they conform to? Infinite planets are circling those stars. Why do these orbits exist? And why does this behavior show up in the circling of electrons around their nuclei? Why do some things exist as light and others as water or gases and yet others as solids or earth?

These substances can't shape themselves because they have no will. Certainly, an intelligent designer (namely, God) is a very reasonable explanation versus random chance and impersonal natural forces.

Inanimate energy or matter does not have creative abilities by itself, but living beings do. The God of the Bible is repeatedly called "the living God." The ability to organize energy and matter into a higher form is clearly a property of living things. These organisms consume resources, grow and replicate. Whether it's a microscopic cell, a plant, or an animal, they ingest lower forms of energy and matter as food that actually becomes part of the being itself. These kinds of organizational abilities are not present in inanimate energy or matter. Therefore, scientific theories clearly fall short of explaining how life began.

---

[22] *Merriam-Webster Dictionary*, "entropy," accessed January 8, 2026, charlesmastroni.com/entropy.

A rock has no initiative, affinity, energy or ability to organize itself into life. It is just a rock. Rocks have the characteristics of texture, hardness and weight. Light has the properties of speed, energy, color and frequency. But neither of these has any organizational qualities of its own. Attributing self-organizing abilities to energy or matter is a completely unproven assumption.

Light does not possess the initiative to become alive. It just zooms at light speed. Soil cannot become a plant. However, a plant, being alive, does have the self-organizational ability to convert sunlight and soil-based nutrients into itself. It grows, absorbs nutrients, receives light, and orients itself toward the sun. One could say that a plant does have the initiative, ability and affinity to turn soil, water and light into itself. But that's because a plant is living.

Science's claim that a plant or a single cell came from the ability of energy and matter to organize themselves is contrary to common sense and everything empirically demonstrated in nature. Living entities can affect and organize energy and matter, not the other way around. However, the living God has the power to exist and to form and shape the universe, as well as the ability, knowledge and will to create all forms of life.

There is a clear demarcation between living things and nonliving energy and matter. Yet science cannot explain how living entities came into existence except by fallaciously assuming matter has the capacity to organize itself into life. Scientists often do this by extrapolating Darwin's theory of survival to energy and matter, even though his theory specifically pertains to living organisms and their initiative, ability or desire to survive. However, he never claimed this quality for inanimate materials because they don't have it.

Yet our children are being taught this as truth in response to their desire to know where everything comes from. This scientific conclusion is the secular belief that forms the child's mind, and therefore the most fundamental aspects of their worldview. In the TAKES model, this translates to a theology that puts forth that there is no God, an anthropology that people evolved from animals and are only animals themselves, a knowledge of the truth that says there is no higher intelligence than humans, an ethical framework that espouses survival of the fittest, and a salvation creed that there is not necessarily an afterlife.

The belief that life can spontaneously erupt from energy and matter with no outside influence is couched in scientific prose by saying we can't see the phenomenon because it happened over millennia. The false circular logic goes like this: "Well, it is here. So it must have happened by chance over millions and billions of years."

Chance is not a cause but a measure of probability. It creates nothing.[23] Substances and life are the result of specific causes. Their existence does not prove they resulted from randomness. This logic is as absurd as claiming that, since automobiles exist, they must have just happened. In other words, energy and matter just made themselves into a car from a pile of metal, rubber, gasoline and batteries with no human interference. The simplest cell is infinitely more complex than an automobile or a plane. So I ask you, what is the probability that the universe and life were caused by an intelligent being like God versus just happening by accident?

Science seems to need to explain away any supreme intelligence or supernatural cause for the existence of this very ordered universe. As a result, intelligent design is controversial in the scientific community and is not included in many school curricula worldwide, while in the US, intelligent design is banned from public school curricula. Again, these mind-shaping truths affect children, and rather than being taught a variety of prevailing thoughts and given the chance to determine for themselves which is true, most aren't ever aware there are alternative explanations for how life came to be. One truth or another will shape our world because beliefs shape people.

Scientific theories of origin lead children to believe there is no God. If existence—theirs, their parents', or the world's—does

---

[23] R. C. Sproul, *Chosen by God* (Peabody, MA: Hendrickson Publishers, 2010), 262.

not have any supernatural cause, then there is no need for any religion at all and no reason to seek meaning in religious teachings. Science eliminates the need for God's objective framework of truth, knowledge, beliefs and morals. It then supplies its own rationale for existence, but offers no basis for moral living, unless you believe survival of the fittest is best for humanity.

Most religions promote what they define as good behavior and discourage what they believe is evil or harmful. But what happens when science and culture tell our children (and us) that there is no God? The inevitable conclusion of this train of thought is that there is no supernatural being that we answer to and that we are not required to choose good over evil. Our only purpose is to survive and contribute to the gene pool.

Because the majority of the scientific community cannot accept the supernatural or that there may be a mind behind the existing universe, it ignores this idea. This is the outcome of the Enlightenment's claim that rational thought is the best determiner of truth. Therefore, according to science, the human mind is the ultimate mind. This is willful ignorance, in my opinion. It continues to look for the cause while steadfastly ignoring the possibility of intelligent design by God even though it is the most likely cause of all that exists. Therefore, our current secular culture has a bias against God as the supernatural intelligence behind the creation of the universe and humankind.

This means, dear reader, that if you live in the Western world, you have been steeped in this culture, and this exact bias is ingrained in your thinking. It affects who we are and how we think and feel, and it shapes our values and worldview. Science attempts to give us an alternate truth or reality—one that excludes the necessity for God. And if you accept this view, then he has no claim on you and religion holds no real value. But is this actually true? You may be inclined to deny the existence of God. However, like someone who owes a debt but doesn't feel like repaying it, you just can't simply *ignore* that you owe God for your life, if in fact, he is your Maker.

The Creation of Life

Let's return to the creation of life itself. Since energy and matter don't possess the properties of living things, how did life come to be? As stated above, the cause of existence is outside of time. Classic Christian theology describes these qualities of God: eternal, unchanging, all-knowing, all-powerful, the Creator. God is and causes all things to come into existence because only God has the power of self-existence. As stated above, he told Moses his name is I AM (Exodus 3:14). Traditionally, in Christian teaching, an eternal state of being would be called "spirit." This is different from energy. "God is spirit," according to Jesus in John 4:24.

For Christians, Jews and Muslims, the Creator is God as depicted in the Bible. Others may believe in intelligent design without accepting this moral God. However, if we believe there is no Creator who designed the universe, then we have to invent our own belief system, because we cannot function in the world without it.

Let's address this point as it applies to the other great modern theory of life, Darwinism. Since science can only deal with the natural world, researchers have gone to great lengths to ignore the possibility of supernatural explanations because this conflicts with their worldview. They focus solely on natural causes that don't explain the existence of the universe or life. The scientific theory of our origins boils down to this: *somehow,* a single cell happened in some kind of primordial soup,[24] which they speculate existed billions of years ago. Of course, they can't prove that because they weren't there. By chance, in this soup of organic material, at some point over millions of years, a cell became alive. And this one cell or many cells *somehow* became alive and evolved into the

---

[24] Scripps Research Institute, "Primordial Soup: Scientists Discover New 'Origins of Life' Chemical Reactions," *Sci Tech Daily*, July 29, 2022, charlesmastroni.com/primordial.

tremendous diversity of plant and animal life we have on our little planet Earth.

Since scientists claim to know how life originated, why don't they just recreate life? If they are so certain, can't they reproduce the process and make a living cell from scratch? A key step in proving a hypothesis is the ability to replicate results. Now, I don't mean to start with a dirty beaker with a cell or two in it. Dear scientists, I challenge you to produce life from the completely inanimate matter that you claim existed millions of years ago. If you can't create life in this manner, then you don't know how it originated, and you don't have a basis for eliminating God as the Creator.

If you think this is an unfair request, consider this example. I worked in carpentry and construction for many years. If you give me the raw materials, I can build a functional house. In the same way, researchers have all the inanimate, inorganic materials at their disposal. Science claims to know and teaches the rest of us that life originated from such a combination of nonliving raw substances. Therefore, it should be possible to take these chemicals and recreate the conditions to make a living cell.

Does it seem likely that all this diverse existence came about through accidental mutations and environmental changes? Look at the overwhelming variety of life on this planet: amoebas, elephants, bacteria, redwood trees, paramecia, whales, yeast, tigers and everything in between. Science would have us believe that all this came about by accident with no intelligent designer, no supernatural causes, no God.

Virtually all living cells have DNA, RNA or both. However, even if there are rare exceptions, these are still fundamentally different from inanimate energy and matter. All living cells will have the defining characteristics of life: they consume resources, metabolize and reproduce.

Now, DNA and RNA are molecules that hold the code of life. Virtually all known organisms rely on one or both. Mathematicians have calculated that it is virtually impossible for even a single strand of these genetic materials to come into existence accidentally, let alone an entire living cell. According to the standard mathematics of probability, DNA is impossible to create by chance. It has been estimated that there is less than 1 chance in 10 to the 109,938 power that a typical protein needed for life could have originated randomly. This is the equivalent of winning the Powerball 12,996 times in a row.[25] And every cell, even the simplest one, has DNA or RNA. Not only that, but they consume resources, respire, grow and reproduce themselves. This requires a complex intercellular system of organelles and processes, which is referred to as "the irreducible complexity of cells." But science explains away the supernatural origin of the universe and life with the magic wand of millions and billions of years, and *somehow*, it happened by chance.

Here are some relatable examples for those of us who are not scientists. If you put your laundry into a dryer, how many times would you have to run it in order for your clothes to come out perfectly folded, buttoned-up, unwrinkled, stacked and ready to be put away? The answer is an infinite number of times, and it still wouldn't happen.

If you went into a junkyard with unlimited amounts of dynamite or a million giant mixers and randomly blew up or jumbled up piles of metal, fuels and rubber a million billion times, would you ever produce a perfectly functioning car? Yet this is basically what science claims.

It is like the axiom, "If you put a million monkeys in a room with a million typewriters, eventually one will produce the complete works of Shakespeare." No, they wouldn't! When this kind of reasoning is combined with Darwin's theory, science makes a monkey out of you.

Do metal and rubber have any initiative to organize themselves into a car (or an airplane or a complex machine) without a designer?

---

[25] Otangelo Grasso, "Let's Throw Mathematical Light on the Origin of Life," *Evolution News & Science Today*, December 15, 2024, charlesmastroni.com/lifeorigins.

The answer is, of course, no. Neither do elements in a primordial soup. And life is trillions of times harder to produce than a machine. It is so much more miraculous than that. No amount of random jumbling and combining of elements could ever result in life.

Anyone who has marveled at the wonders of the animal kingdom—a whale, lion, butterfly or the complexity of a single leaf—will intuitively know that life is no accident. Are you an accident? Science is essentially telling us we are.

The apostle Paul says in Romans 1:19–20, "For what can be known about God is plain to them, because God has shown it to them. For his invisible attributes, namely, his eternal power and divine nature, have been clearly perceived, ever since the creation of the world, in the things that have been made. So they are without excuse."

Science has a passionate romance
that the universe happened by chance.

There is no great being above us,
no Creator, so don't bother to discuss.

We can't explain existence,
but we are persistent.

Life's origin is another mystery,
but science will discern its history.

Science has the smartest brains,
and yet they still cannot explain,

Where matter comes from, nor a cell or a flower,
but they will not accept a higher power.

God the Creator is the ultimate cause.
He made the world and all natural laws.

The origin of life is the work of His hand.
This should be plain to the mind of man.

What will atheist scientists say
when they meet the Creator at the end of their days?

Since life was created by a supernatural being with intelligence and purpose, the God of the Bible, that means you and I are not random accidents. Our lives have value and meaning gifted to us by our Maker. This is a superior explanation to random chance.

Researchers have managed to clone existing animals and have engineered the birth process with the misnomer of test-tube babies, but these are only alterations of existing processes created by God. They can manipulate life but not create it. They cannot even engineer a single living cell.

When a person is officially declared dead, all the material and DNA are still there. Why can't scientists bring them back to life? Because it is produced by supernatural means that remain beyond them and in the realm of our Creator, God.

Survival of the Fittest

Darwin's theory of evolution is based on the survival of the fittest in response to environmental changes. Variations in the genes of a species are based on gradual, random genetic mutations over millions of years. If the environment changes, these genetic advantages allow the individual to survive and procreate, while those that do not possess the new genetic makeup will die off.

It has been scientifically demonstrated that there is variation within a species, but this does not account for tremendous changes from one species to the next. Look at the features of existing animals that would be disadvantages if they came about gradually, such as the development of wings[26] for prehistoric reptiles and birds. A *functioning* set of wings could not have come into existence through gradual and random genetic mutation. Such creatures actually defy Darwin's theory.

Nonfunctioning wings would be completely disadvantageous to survival if the animal could not fly. Since wings formed from forelimbs using the same bone and skin structure, any kind of

---

[26] Philip Johnson, *Darwin on Trial* (Downers Grove, IL: InterVarsity Press, 2010).

gradual modification would have left the creature more vulnerable and decreased its chances of survival. And the odds of fully functional wings appearing all at once in a single individual by pure chance are astronomically small.

In addition, since reptiles and birds reproduce sexually, one mutant with fully developed wings would not be sufficient because it would die off with that first individual. In fact, there would have to be both a male and a female with this amazing mutation living at the same time, in the same place, in order to produce offspring with fully functioning wings. They would also have to fly with their first mutation in order to gain a competitive advantage. Yet if these mutations were random, why would they happen again?

What are the odds of a random genetic mutation of a male and a female of a species within their same lifetimes with the same anomaly of functioning wings? Astronomical odds squared! No, birds were created as birds.

Another example that defies Darwin's theory of evolution is the beaver. A genetic mutation could not provide them with the innate engineering ability to construct dams at ideal locations, using flexible trees woven together and packed with mud to create an underwater entrance. This reminds me of cartoons from when I was a kid where beavers have blueprints, calculators and hard hats. The idea that random genetic mutations would give them this ability is equally comical. Also, beavers have perfectly designed teeth for chewing and felling small trees, and they select them according to their suitability for the dam. And yes, they have flat tails for paddles that are effective for swimming underwater and also for packing mud into place to waterproof their dams. What series of random genetic mutations could give them all these physiological features combined with the engineering knowledge or inclination to build a dam? Just because beavers are here, it doesn't mean they developed these traits through evolution. The answer is, beavers were created to be beavers.

Even though gradual and random genetic mutations cannot explain the ability of beavers, one might say their brains are more complex, and therefore, they are relatively high on the evolutionary chain as mammals. But what about bees? These insects have much simpler brains. How does one bee genetically mutate with the engineering know-how to create remarkably regular hexagonal cells? In addition, even despite their tiny brains, bees engage in complex behavior. Their survival cannot be attributed to genetic mutations. No, it is eminently more likely that the variety of life as we know it was designed by a supernatural intelligence. And I maintain that is the God of the Bible.

The Effects of Enlightenment

Until modern science became such an extensive influence in our worldview, virtually all people groups and cultures believed in a supernatural cause for creation. Science and existential philosophies have steadfastly limited themselves to the natural world to the detriment of our souls. According to Enlightenment philosophy, human reason was considered the primary means for discovering truth and understanding reality, often taking precedence over tradition, religion and superstition. In other words, if our best minds cannot understand or know something, then it can't be true or real. Many consider Enlightenment philosophy to be an evolution of the human mind. However, this eliminates instinctive knowledge.

We don't invent the truth. It is discovered or revealed to people. Great thinkers and even many scientists describe their newfound knowledge as coming to them in an inspiration, revelation or even a dream, like Einstein's realization of relativity.[27] Objective truth and knowledge come from outside our minds, and beliefs that are held as truth are taken from our life experiences. Modern science holds that there are only natural causes for all existing phenomena,

---

[27] Paul Sutter, "How Einstein's Daydream of Light Created Relativity," *Universe Today*, November 9, 2023, charlesmastroni.com/einstein.

and if man can't explain or understand it, then it can't be claimed as knowledge. But Shakespeare in *Hamlet* would certainly disagree. "There are more things in heaven and earth, Horatio, than are dreamt of in your philosophy."[28] Was Shakespeare unenlightened? Were Newton, DaVinci and Bach without reason and understanding? They all believed in God.

Whether the human mind is actually the final determiner of what is real and true is neatly summed up in the classic riddle, "If a tree falls in the forest and no one is around to hear it, does it make a sound?" The answer is a resounding *yes!* The tree fell and crashed noisily. Even if no one is around to hear it, the objective truth is it still dropped, and that makes a loud racket.

The fact this question is even asked is profoundly telling of the arrogance of the human mind. We don't see, hear or understand the whole universe completely. Does that mean it is not real? We don't even see everything in the ocean. Does that mean these objects don't exist? We don't see thoughts or emotions, and we don't understand where they come from. Does that mean they are not real? The "God is dead" philosophy of Friedrich Nietzsche and the existential philosophies of Jean-Paul Sartre may say there is no supernatural because they don't perceive it, but that does not mean they are right.

Like the riddle of the fallen tree, these philosophical trains of thought lead down the track to the conclusion that human beings are independent of God and we make our reality and meaning without him. Since he makes us free, we can invent our own meaning and ignore him. But is this objectively true? The universe and humanity have meaning and purpose because of God, who created both. To find complete truth, we need the supernatural, which means we need God.

---

[28] William Shakespeare, *Hamlet*, in *The Globe Illustrated Shakespeare: The Complete Works Annotated*, ed. Howard Staunton, illus. John Gilbert (New York: Greenwich House, 1983), 1.5.167–68.

Evolution or the Supernatural

Historically, instinctively and with fundamental common sense, humanity believed in the supernatural and in life after death. They believed there were better and worse outcomes for our eternal fate. They worshipped idols or the God of the Bible. And they held that we (humankind) are eternal—specifically, that we have an eternal spirit (soul) and we are not purely physical entities that die and cease to be. Despite the fact that you can't prove God's existence scientifically, you cannot disprove his existence either.

Religious beliefs include moral frameworks leading to a rewarding afterlife. These have provided a tremendous benefit to civilization because there is an authority above us that we must answer to. We self-correct when making decisions because our actions have eternal consequences. This correction is absent from science and much current philosophy influencing our worldview. And a no-consequences belief system eventually removes any moral restrictions to uncivilized behavior. This is likely why so many young people are drawn to anarchy, a motivating philosophy that rejects all authority except one's own and that of like-minded individuals. Oddly enough, anarchists often seek to impose their own rules on those who do not share their worldview. In many cases, their protests move beyond persuasion and turn to violence against any form of governing they oppose.

The effect of the theories of evolution and the Big Bang on our culture is as harmful as it is pervasive. Since the public generally accepts these theories, this has affected our society because it influences our worldview. In the West, only science's explanation for our origin is taught as true knowledge in most schools. In the US, religious instruction is banned in public education.

Even though the public probably has never read Darwin's *On the Origin of Species*, I maintain that the word *evolution* has become part of our belief system, shaping our minds. This theory subtly includes the idea that everything automatically improves over time since matter somehow became alive and we evolved from simple cells. This leads to the assumption that we all are better than our ancestors, which is how the evolution thought train goes down the tracks and becomes a mind-shaping belief that couldn't be further from the truth. But nothing gets organized, nothing improves, nothing develops without a mind and intentionality behind it.

We routinely hear phrases like the evolution of the personal computer, of modern science, of the cell phone, and of the minivan. Even personal growth is described as an individual evolution: developing into a better version of oneself. Of course, all of these have intelligent designers behind them. But the belief that the word *evolution* is linked to automatic improvement is a result of the influence of Darwinism and the Big Bang theory.

With this concept, young minds are bound to draw faulty conclusions. History doesn't matter because everything is better now than it was before. People are better, wiser and more moral. This belief allows every new psychological and scientific theory to be seen as an improvement. But the fact is, only technology has developed. Human beings have not.

We are every bit as amoral as we have been throughout history, and the idea that anything we think is better than what came before produces a self-righteous superiority. We will have no respect for history and won't learn from it because it has nothing to teach us. Educators shaped by this belief know better than all who came before. Children can think they are morally evolved compared to their parents and feel justified in dishonoring them.

With this mindset, there will be no cultural growth of understanding, which will lead to repeating history's mistakes on a grander scale with more powerful technology. Humanity has not demonstrated it has the wisdom, morality or self-control to handle the club or the sword. We now have the atomic bomb and are altering our genetics. And unless a different worldview takes hold of our culture, we are creating this world, and our youth must live in it.

When you combine the notion of Darwinism's survival of the fittest with Nietzsche's will to power (a desire for domination or mastery over others, oneself or the environment), it approaches a perfect storm of violence. These two beliefs have no basis of morality or kindness and no restraint on the dark side of human nature. Without a moral foundation, there is no right and wrong, no good and evil—only power and survival. This system eliminates mental illness or physical weakness, as it did in Nazi Germany. As previously mentioned, though, rightly practiced religion does have such restraints, based on real truth, and offers a morality that leads to civilized life. The failures of organized religions are well-documented. However, this is the result of misapplied doctrine and not the intention of the founders, particularly Jesus.

What do you believe? Does God exist or not? If yes, what is the truth about God, and what has he given to humankind? If one decides or believes there is no God, what is the result?

Science has repeated that God is not needed to explain our origin.

But science can't specifically prove it scientifically, much to their chagrin.

Philosophy says God is dead, but they do not know for certain.

I shudder to see their faces when it's time to close life's curtain.

Why are they so dedicated to making God antiquated?

Part Two. Secular Worldviews

CHAPTER 6

A Further Exploration of Worldviews

We previously touched on the theology of a godless worldview and the resulting anthropology that forms from science, the Big Bang theory, and Darwinism. And we examined some effects of these beliefs on one's worldview, which shapes our very self. Let's continue comparing and contrasting worldviews using the TAKES model.

If our theology includes the Creator, our life is intentional and intelligent. We have a unique purpose. Without him, our existence is random. We have no real purpose to our lives other than surviving well and procreating. With Darwinism, we are no better or different from any other animal as far as our right to exist and our place in the world. Many animal rights groups think exactly this. Their anthropology of what you and I are says we are just one animal among many.

> PETA opposes speciesism, a human-supremacist worldview, and focuses its attention on the four areas in which the largest numbers of animals suffer the most intensely for the longest periods of time: in laboratories, in the food industry,

> in the clothing trade, and in the entertainment business. We also work on a variety of other issues, including the cruel killing of rodents, birds, and other animals who are often considered "pests" as well as cruelty to domesticated animals.[29]

God gave us responsibility and dominion over creation to treat it kindly and use it gratefully and wisely. However, some animal rights groups hold extreme views that justify attacks on other humans, such as medical researchers, and spray-painting fur coats.[30] They define the mistreatment of animals as murder. You may have seen the slogan, "Fur is murder." While it can be argued that harvesting fur is unnecessarily cruel to animals, murder is the wanton killing of a human being. However, speciesism believes otherwise and, according to its worldview, does not differentiate between people and animals. While the Christian worldview condemns the mistreatment of animals, it does not reduce human beings to mere members of the animal kingdom.

Extreme groups like Population Connection advocate for zero population growth.[31] They want to control the size of the human race. They have curricula for primary and secondary schools to indoctrinate young minds with their truth (knowledge), all supposedly for the greater good of the survival of the planet and humanity. This outlook amounts to worshipping the Earth itself as a kind of goddess whose well-being we must serve. This is basically their theology and anthropology. They believe their environmental models are correct and that population limits are

---

[29] "Animals Are Not Ours," PETA, accessed January 8, 2026, charlesmastroni.com/peta.

[30] Grace Hwang, "Examining Extremism: Violent Animal Rights Extremists," Center for Strategic & International Studies, August 20, 2021, charlesmastroni.com/extremism.

[31] "Our Mission and Goals," Population Connection, accessed January 8, 2026, charlesmastroni.com/populationconnection.

necessary, and they wholeheartedly believe they know what is best for the planet they revere. By contrast, the Christian worldview holds that God is the Creator and sustainer of the world, which is upheld by his power, not by human efforts to control the global population size.

God as our designer is the foundation of solid, reliable, absolute truth. We have something real to believe in. With a godless worldview, people invent their own truth, which is actually playing God. Even when their beliefs do not equal reality, they persist, wanting it to be real. And if they organize into groups, they try to force their imagined reality onto everyone else.

The Creator knows what is good for people and what hurts them. In the secular worldview, acceptable and permissible actions are only what people agree upon in a society. With God, our Maker determines morality. As a result, communities work properly together, based on objective values. This leads to right behaviors.

Without God, the source of right and wrong lies with human wisdom and is determined by the cultural worldview we grew up with. Morality becomes subjective, depending on who is in power and who is influencing culture. People are essentially self-centered and self-serving. Christian teaching refers to this as the fallen state of humanity. Essentially, we tend to believe and do what is best for us and acceptable to our peers. In our fallen state, our understanding of what is good leans heavily on what we see as beneficial for ourselves individually or as a collective "we."

Societies and interest groups behave in the same manner, based on what they perceive to be the collective good of like-minded people with common self-interests. These groups share a worldview, whether true or false. But when different factions push for competing laws, truths and morals—each seeking power to establish its own version of what is true and right—this is hardly a path to objective truth and good.

As should be self-evident, a worldview and belief in a divine creator differs dramatically from a secular worldview. However, what the majority of people believe shapes societies. This affects the decisions of individuals, organizations and governments, ultimately determining the quality of life for the individual and the community. Some examples follow.

The Value of Human Life

Since God is our Creator, humanity owes him acknowledgment and gratitude for our existence, both individually and collectively. We did not create ourselves, and no one is an accident. All people ultimately belong to their Creator, and every human life has value because each one was intentionally designed to fulfill God's purpose. There never was, and never will be, another you. Our meaning cannot be found apart from communication with our Maker. Without him, under Social Darwinism, human life has no objective value beyond what others assign to it, and our lives have no more importance than that of an animal. But under the Christian worldview, every person, man or woman, bears the image of God and is therefore cherished, from the least to greatest.

Social Darwinism dictates that we must compete to survive. Our value is judged by our usefulness and superiority to others. What can we do for people? How attractive are we? Do others admire or respect us? How powerful or famous are we? Are we rich and successful? These are the criteria that determine a person's status and value on both micro and macro levels: from family, to groups, to communities, to nations. When one's status is gone, one's value vanishes.

Look at how powerful people throughout history have treated the powerless. Most people know this is wrong, yet neither Darwinism, the Big Bang, nor science offers a solid foundation for valuing all people equally. At best, they provide a rationale for justifying who we consider to be "superior," according to whatever standards a society adopts. Though rarely acknowledged, these belief systems devalue those deemed "inferior," according to the person's qualities. This is rarely, if ever, admitted, but the result of Social Darwinism can easily lead to the justification of eliminating those deemed to be weak, harmful, undesirable or evil from the gene pool. If such thinking is accepted as truth, it will inevitably shape and distort a culture's morals.

This is how progressive cancel-culture activists justify themselves. They believe they are entitled to strip the rights of those they deem harmful or undesirable, and they instill fear in others so the world conforms to their vision. In doing so, they demand that humanity reflects their image rather than God's. Social Darwinism easily justifies cancel culture and even genocide. The Nazi's belief in Aryan superiority and the supposed evil of the Jewish people was a lie. Yet with enough propaganda, people believed it and, once it was enforced, it led to genocide. Cancel culture today destroys jobs, ruins reputations, and brands those who disagree as evil. The Nazis killed millions of Jews. However, both belief systems are the result of Darwinian thinking. The difference between them is not in the underlying mindset, but in the degree of power held.

What do science and post-Christian philosophy offer as foundational truth in this key area? If life just happened by chance and we are the result of random mutations, what value does a human being have? As for communal life, they offer nothing but subjective morality.

First, science and philosophy are limited to human minds, whether high or low in intelligence. However, many people who are considered geniuses have been power hungry or even plainly evil (for example, Napoleon Bonaparte, Adolf Hitler, Vladimir Lenin, Julius Caesar, Genghis Khan). Brainpower does not guarantee goodness or morality. Like technology, intelligence can be used for good or evil. It is also no guarantee of benevolent wisdom.

Look at post-Christian philosophy and science. The field of science offers nothing in the way of wisdom or morals. And post-Christian philosophy doesn't offer much more help on the subject.

The philosopher David Hume states that reason is the "slave of the passions."[32] If Hume is correct, then we'd better believe in God because we need the moral foundation he provides, not one based on human passions or reason. While individual scientists may have a high moral standard, science as it is taught to our children does not reflect that. And it doesn't recognize God as the answer to how we came to be.

In another example, Nietzsche's philosophy of the will to power may be rooted in human intelligence and seeks to explain why some individuals achieved great historical success as so-called supermen. Yet it ultimately reinforces the notion that might makes right—and we know that is not true, I hope. History has produced geniuses such as Julius Caesar, Napoleon Bonaparte, Albert Einstein and Stephen Hawking, but who provides the truth for living—defining right and wrong, good and evil?

By definition, wisdom must be grounded in truth and reality. The Bible presents a Christian worldview of what it means to live with knowledge and understanding. It contains hundreds of passages that reflect on the nature of sound judgment. King Solomon, who is historically regarded as a man of remarkable wisdom, wrote the majority of Proverbs. The Psalms and Proverbs preserve many of these enduring teachings.

- "The fear of the Lord is the beginning of knowledge, but fools despise wisdom and instruction" (Proverbs 1:7 NIV).

- "The beginning of wisdom is this: Get wisdom. Though it cost all you have, get understanding" (Proverbs 4:7 NIV).

- "The fear of the Lord is the beginning of wisdom, and knowledge of the Holy One is understanding" (Proverbs 9:10 NIV).

---

[32] Rachel Cohon, "Hume's Moral Philosophy," Stanford University, updated August 20, 2018, charlesmastroni.com/hume.

Note that the word *fear* is also translated as "awe." Understanding comes from what God has revealed to us as rules for living because he is the Creator. He knows what is right and wrong and how he intended everything to be, including people. Yet fools despise knowledge from God, according to Solomon.

Christian belief holds that God created the universe and everything in it, including man and woman. Therefore, he has a legitimate claim on every individual. As the designer and creator of all that is, God sets the laws of physics and of life, including how we should live, what constitutes good and evil, and what is right and wrong. He has the right to judge if an individual or a society is complying with his design or not because he is the source of objective truth, knowledge and wisdom.

To be wise, the first truth to know and believe is that God is. God exists. He knows how the world and people are supposed to be because he designed and created us. He formed nature and gave us the ability to know right from wrong and good from evil. Our conscience is not perfect because cultural beliefs may strongly influence us, but it is present as part of our psyche. Christianity calls it a gift of God's grace, so we have a chance at living well and choosing good over evil.

God also made people free to obey or disobey, to live rightly or wrongly. He did not make robots but individuals with the ability to choose, even though right and wrong have positive and negative consequences. However, God lets our choices affect us because he made us free. When we obey, it is not dictatorial but voluntary, out of gratitude for our very life. God is also free and can choose. He tells Moses, "I will have mercy on whom I will have mercy, and I will have compassion on whom I will have compassion" (Exodus 33:19 NIV). To hear the Creator or accept any blessing he may have for you, you must first believe God exists.

For moral guidance, science writers and documentary producers often look to the animal kingdom. The internet and television channels like Animal Planet and Discovery are steeped in pictures of wild animals tenderly caring for their young, hunting prey, and narrowly escaping predators. And there is no shortage of images of the cutest newborn creatures. But when it comes to morals and values, what guidance does nature really offer? For marriage, should we take our cues from the black widow spider that kills her mate or from the loyal penguins who mate for life? Even among mammals, survival often takes precedence over sentiment. Some eat their young if they are hungry enough, and primates may kill the offspring of rivals to further their chances of mating. Is this the standard we want shaping our view of life and morality?

According to Darwinism, the weak will be eliminated from the gene pool. As one writer proposed, when we look to nature for moral guidance, the lessons all depend on where you point the binoculars (my paraphrase).[33] If nature is your guide to morality, then there is no motivation to help the poor and feed the hungry. Even with all its institutional faults, Christianity has been truly giving over the centuries when it comes to supporting those in need. But with Darwinism as your guide, the poor are weak and drag the rest of us down. What source offers the better morality for the human race: God or scientific consensus?

Our society, influenced by genetic knowledge, is now screening for birth defects, often leading to decisions to abort a baby. This thinking is an obvious effect of Social Darwinism (survival of the fittest), anticipating the impact such a defect will have on the child's life and their parents'. People base their judgments of what is desirable or not on their own belief system, which may or may not include God.

Technology has now given us designer babies. This is clearly an effect of a secular worldview, ignoring God in favor of customizing a baby for oneself. People without God believe they are only answerable to themselves or society. Science believes everything is

---

[33] Daniel Callahan, "Can Nature Serve as a Moral Guide?," *The Hastings Center Report* 26, No. 6, (November–December 1996):20–22, charlesmastroni.com/naturesmorality.

within its purview to manipulate. But what if we do have to answer to God, our Maker?

This brings us back to the central question: What is the truth? What is real? And what forms our minds? Objective truth is not invented but discovered. We don't decide what is true. We acknowledge and accept it if we want to remain sane and wise.

"So God created man in his own image, in the image of God he created him; male and female he created them" (Genesis 1:27). I claim this is objective truth. And we all have value in God's eyes because of it: all races, men and women, young and old, the weak and the strong, the privileged and the poor, no matter your status in society.

What do you believe? And is it the truth?

Spiritual Roadblocks to the Truth

Why do we have such a hard time recognizing the truth? The Bible explains the reason. But first, it is important to clarify what is meant by *spiritual roadblocks*. These are not intellectual shortcomings or a lack of information. Rather, they are deep-seated tendencies within human nature that make us resistant to the truth. Scripture teaches that humanity's struggle began when we learned to doubt God's word, question his goodness, trust our own judgment as equal to—or even greater than—his, and disobey his commandments. Since that time, these inclinations have shaped how we think, what we believe, and whom we trust.

The story in Genesis 3 explains not only how deception entered the world but also why it still has such a powerful influence on us today. In the biblical account, the serpent represents the embodiment of spiritual evil, a corrupt angel who led a rebellion against God and lied to humanity from the start. (The Bible contains parables, prophecy, symbolism and analogy written in both prose and poetry, so it should not be read in a strictly literal sense.) In Scripture, Adam and Eve are clearly depicted as the origin of humanity. They knew only God and each other, and they were living in his created order before they faced the temptation of the forbidden fruit, which contained the knowledge of evil.

Scripture explains why humanity fell from its original state and why we have such a difficult time accepting truth.

> Now the serpent was more crafty than any other beast of the field that the Lord God had made. He said to the woman, "Did God actually say, 'You shall not eat of any tree in the garden'?" And the woman said to the serpent, "We may eat of the fruit of the trees in the garden, but God said, 'You shall not eat of the fruit of the tree that is in the midst of the garden, neither shall you touch it, lest you die.'" But the serpent said to the woman, "You will not surely die. For God knows that when you eat of it your eyes will be opened, and you will be like God, knowing good and evil." So when the woman saw that the tree was good for food, and that it was a delight to the eyes, and that the tree was to be desired to make one wise, she took of its fruit and ate, and she also gave some to her husband who was with her, and he ate. (Genesis 3:1–6)

These few verses in Genesis have been the source of many books, so I will keep my explanation short. What is not debatable is: Genesis describes when and how lies and evil entered humanity. Prior to eating the fruit, they only knew good. Before their disobedience, they walked in perfect harmony with creation and in communion with God, with no fear of him. We face roadblocks to accepting the truth because we are compromised by the lies resonating within us.

The first lie was the questioning of God's command by the serpent: "Did God actually say, 'You shall not eat of any tree in the garden'?" This was the first spiritual roadblock—casting doubt on whether God had truly spoken and whether his word could be trusted. While he did not forbid this, there was one tree he commanded them not to eat from. He had told Adam and Eve earlier in Genesis 2:16–17 (NIV):

> And the Lord God commanded the man, "You are free to eat from any tree in the garden; but you must not eat from the tree of the knowledge of good and evil, for when you eat from it you will certainly die."

Adam and Eve were free to make their own choices, but they were told not to partake of the forbidden fruit. Yet they did anyway. Disobedience is the second spiritual roadblock.

Eve, with Adam right there listening, engaged with the spirit who rebelled against God, and Adam did nothing. She didn't fall for this lie at first and attempted to correct the serpent.

> And the woman said to the serpent, "We may eat of the fruit of the trees in the garden, but God said, 'You shall not eat of the fruit of the tree that is in the midst of the garden, neither shall you touch it, lest you die'" (Genesis 3:2–3).

Next, the serpent blatantly called God a liar by saying, "You will not surely die." But don't we all die? Adam and Eve didn't die immediately. However, this is when death entered humanity.

When Adam and Eve disobeyed the God they knew, they believed the spirit of evil, accepting lies as part of their beliefs. This event is called the "fall of humanity" in Christian teaching. This major roadblock in our nature continues to obstruct us, preventing us from recognizing truth. These same tendencies— doubting God's word, questioning his goodness, elevating human judgment, and defying his word—remain in us today.

By lying, this spirit downplayed the consequences of the forbidden fruit and promised great benefits for disobeying God's instruction. "For God knows that when you eat of it your eyes will be opened, and you will be like God, knowing good and evil" (v. 5). Here the lie deepened. Not only was God's goodness questioned, but the forbidden fruit was presented as something to be desired rather than something to be protected from. Adam and Eve then internalized this lie, and it became part of human nature and another roadblock to understanding God's truth. When we doubt his goodness, we don't seek his wisdom.

Under the influence of the serpent's lies, Adam and Eve ate the forbidden fruit, which became part of their being. A dark spiritual side in us now knows evil, not by God's doing but by our own. Human nature was altered from being formed in the image of God into becoming disbelievers of his good intentions, who long for equal status with him. Humanity believed they were wise—just as wise as God. And our fall was by our own choice, ignoring his explicit warning. These are our spiritual roadblocks to the truth and to God.

The same pattern of doubts and lies continues in our spirits. In modern secular culture, most prominently in the West, many consider Christianity to be a myth, and God is believed to be antiquated and irrelevant, optional at best and harmful at worst. We trust ourselves more than we trust God and believe our wisdom is equal to his. Science and human reason are considered the preeminent determiners of truth. Basically, if science has not proven it, then we cannot claim it is true. This is another expression of the cultural belief that human reasoning alone is sufficient to determine truth.

Cultural trends have made us question even our own instinctive knowledge. For example, scientific studies now show that sunshine or a lack of it affects our mood. This was determined by exposing people to sunlight to see if chemicals were released and in what amounts.[34] Do we really need a scientific study to know that sunshine lifts our spirits? John Denver told us this when he sang "Sunshine on My Shoulders." He knew this without a study, and so do we. Yet our culture increasingly hesitates to trust even obvious truths unless they are validated by human authority.

This is on a par with the discovery that hungry people feel better when they eat. Perhaps we need a government-funded study to tell us this is true, or maybe we can trust our common sense.

Believing humanity's wisdom can be equal to God's leads to dramatic departures from the truth. For example, the quasi-sciences of sociology and psychology tell us that people change genders fluidly and the physical reality of our bodies means nothing. They want us to believe all gender traits are the result of socialization and that there are no natural differences between male and female. This flies in the face of the intuitive knowledge of every culture, from tribal to sophisticated, throughout time, as reflected in virtually all classic art and literature. Yet these quasi-sciences say that history is wrong and they know the truth: gender is fluid and separate from our physical self.

Science says there are genders endless
In buying clothes for one, you will spend less.

    Nature says there are only two.
    To make more people like me and you.

        Will Dad become Mom and Mom become Dad?
        Won't this confuse the lass and the lad?

            Science says there are more genders than two.
            Will you let them make a fool out of you?

---

[34] Shia T. Kent, Leslie A. McClure, William L. Crosson, et al., "Effect of sunlight exposure on cognitive function among depressed and non-depressed participants: a REGARDS cross-sectional study," *Environ Health* 8, no. 34 (2009), doi.org/10.1186/1476-069X-8-34.

I categorize psychology and sociology as quasi-sciences because the study of the human psyche and societies is not as mathematically precise and definitive as physics and chemistry. Yet large percentages of the public accept proclamations of experts in these disciplines as absolute truth. Governments change policies and enact laws based on academic experts, and the news services love to jump on controversial revelations of science as long as a PhD endorses them. This is the roadblock of humanity believing it is as wise as God or maybe wiser.

The mind-expanding drug culture of the 1960s is another example of a false promise, very similar to the serpent's lie of knowledge and wisdom. Dr. Timothy Leary, the high priest of LSD,[35][36] claimed these drugs expanded your mind, gave you insight, and inspired your music and art. Are psychedelic drugs bad for you? According to Dr. Leary, no, they're not harmful. Instead, they make you a wiser, better, more insightful, and energetic version of yourself. Like the serpent's promise, these drugs offer wisdom without obedience and insight without truth. This sounds like another forbidden fruit, and our fallen human nature is very susceptible to such lies.

Common sense tells us that hallucinogenic drugs lead to hallucinations, to things that are not real or true. Even some prescription medications can be addictive. These iconic drugs of the 1960s and beyond led to insanity and delusions among users, as well as damaging genetic mutations in the children of LSD-addicted parents. Such dependencies ruined many lives and resulted in an increase in crime.

People sometimes believe indulging will make others accept you and see you as cool. At first, cocaine was touted as nonaddictive.

---

[35] Leah Silverman, "Inside The Strange Journey Of Timothy Leary, From Harvard Professor To 'The High Priest Of LSD,'" *All That's Interesting*, updated March 26, 2025, charlesmastroni.com/leary.
[36] Lysergic acid diethylamide, otherwise known as LSD, is a potent psychedelic drug known for its intense effects on thoughts, emotions and sensory perception.

Supposedly, it would make you more alert and energetic. Not only was it prevalent on the street, but it also made it "big time" to Wall Street. And the promise of opioids is peace, euphoria and escape from reality. The sales pitch here sounds a lot like the lies the serpent told in Genesis. "No, drugs won't hurt you. They're actually good for you. You will be a better version of yourself. Ignore the laws. They're just there to keep this wonderful substance from you, to keep you from enjoying life."

Humanity at its origin should have known it couldn't be equal to God. And I believe at least a vestige of this truth still remains in all of us. We did not create ourselves, the world or all that is in it. And we don't yet know how nature works or everything that is in space, the oceans, or even our own subconscious. Yet we will make up our beliefs as we see fit because we think we know good and evil just as well as God does. The biblical account clearly says Adam and Eve disobeyed God before they had any offspring. This disobedience was passed on to their children, infecting all of humanity with these lies from the beginning of the human race. We have all been contaminated with evil, which is always present in us, even when our intentions are good. It hides in the shadows of our subconscious. In the end, the same four roadblocks persist— doubting God's word, questioning his goodness, trusting ourselves more than him, and being disobedient to him.

God's Provision of Truth

Since these roadblocks to truth can be difficult for people to navigate, God has left a record of our origin to last through many generations and cultures. Here is the classic Christian teaching, according to the Bible.

God revealed the creation story to Moses, the human author of Genesis, through a combination of prose and imagery designed to stand the test of time. It also had to be able to touch people at their core, where beliefs are formed.

To give Genesis a fair reading, one must realize an infinitely intelligent God is revealing truth to finite minds. The message had to endure in a form that would last for centuries, be translatable into countless languages, and be understood by many cultures. Language itself is a limiting factor, as is the capacity of the human mind when compared with God's. We may be made in his image, but we are never his equal.

Creation as described in the first three chapters of Genesis communicates the fundamental truth of our origin. While Genesis is not a scientific exposition, it is true. It was not written to satisfy every curiosity that would ever come up. Instead, it explains fundamental, foundational truths to every generation of humanity in every culture.

Genesis is not a book of paleontology, genetics or physics. Instead, it presents God as the Creator of the heavens and the earth, light and darkness, the sun, moon and stars. He created plants, fish, animals and finally humankind—Adam and Eve. Eve was formed from Adam, signifying the beginning of God's institution of marriage. Male and female were made distinct, yet were meant to reunite in the sexual act to procreate, in direct obedience to God's command to Adam and Eve.

> God blessed them and said to them, "Be fruitful
> and increase in number; fill the earth and subdue
> it. Rule over the fish in the sea and the birds in the
> sky and over every living creature that moves on
> the ground" (Genesis 1:28 NIV).

> That is why a man leaves his father and mother
> and is united with his wife to become one flesh
> (Genesis 2:24 NIV).

God created two sexes only. The natural world consists of two genders throughout humanity and among higher animals. This is objective truth. People can doubt this, but God is clear. Regardless, one article says:

> In today's society, there is a lot of talk about gender, especially among the young generations. But how many genders are there according to science? It's a common misconception that there are only two genders: male and female. But science proves there is actually more. Contrary to sex, gender isn't binary. It's fluid and ever-changing, which means that there are an endless number of possibilities.[37]

God teaches that this is wrong. Plants and animals procreate according to their kind. He designed and created each species. This is a fundamental, mind-shaping truth, and humanity has always empirically seen this. Species reproduce the same species, with few exceptions. The Bible says:

> The land produced vegetation: plants bearing seed according to their kinds and trees bearing fruit with seed in it according to their kinds. And God saw that it was good (Genesis 1:12 NIV).

Genesis 1:20–21 (NIV) goes on to say:

> And God said, "Let the water teem with living creatures, and let birds fly above the earth across the vault of the sky." So God created the great creatures of the sea and every living thing with which the water teems and that moves about in it, according to their kinds, and every winged bird according to its kind. And God saw that it was good.

---

[37] Maria Pengue, "How Many Genders Are There According to Science: Breaking the Myth," Seed Scientific, June 3, 2022, charlesmastroni.com/gendernumber.

Genesis 1:24–25 (NIV) continues:

> And God said, "Let the land produce living creatures according to their kinds: the livestock, the creatures that move along the ground, and the wild animals, each according to its kind." And it was so. God made the wild animals according to their kinds, the livestock according to their kinds, and all the creatures that move along the ground according to their kinds. And God saw that it was good.

Is that not objectively true? This is what has always happened for life to continue and for species to survive.

Again, the Bible is not intended to conform to modern science since God is far superior. The Creator did not describe the origin of the entire universe as a scientific report. Instead, he tells the creation story in a way that cultures across time can understand without any difficulty. By ignoring the possibility of God, modern scientific theories go out of their way to eliminate him from our minds and replace his truth with their own.

Although there are certain crossbreeds, like the mule (a horse and a donkey) and the liger (a lion and a tiger), most are sterile, and they only breed rarely in nature. This is due to the natural order of species created by God. While humanity has intentionally bred and modified plants and animals, these are clear examples of humankind imitating God as a designer. Yet in each of these cases, people are the ones choosing which animals to pair. These are not random mutations that create new species, as Darwin's theory suggests. Despite the variety produced, dogs remain dogs, cats remain cats, horses remain horses, and livestock remain livestock. They all still breed within their own kind to produce fertile offspring.

Over the centuries, even Christian scholars have debated whether the seven days of creation are literal time periods or if they span eons. They argue that since God exists outside of time as an eternal being, his use of "days" could mean eons or it could be a concession to the human understanding of days. Although not every scientific detail is included, Genesis provides a true and realistic worldview that acknowledges God as the Creator, while offering a basic, yet correct, understanding of where we came from.

God doesn't have to prove anything to you or me—we owe him our existence. He formed the heavens and the earth and created us in his image to have a unique, conscious awareness of him and to be in relationship with him. We are made to be his image-bearers in the conduct of our lives.

Did you create or will yourself into being? No, you didn't. Your parents did not invent life by their own will either. You came into being because they engaged in the act of sex and procreated as part of the process designed by God. They did not invent life. They only followed God's created way to make people, you being one.

If our lives depended on our will alone, we would die rather quickly. Do you have to remember to breathe? No, God designed our bodies to do so. What would happen if this bodily function depended on our unflagging attention to remember to inhale and exhale? You and I have no control over our will as we sleep. Even if we could maintain our focus to breathe every second while awake, we would die as soon as we slept.

Do we digest food by the power of our will, knowledge and understanding? No, our bodies were created for us, and we owe God his due. Did you design your eyes to see, or do you simply have sight? The same is true of hearing, smelling, tasting and touching. We do not will ourselves to have any of these abilities. We have them because God made it that way. Life belongs to us only as a gift from him. Therefore, is it right for us to deny his existence? We need to thank him for our very lives.

These are the moral implications of the simple truth that God created us, and we owe our being to him. This is where the Christian stance on the sanctity of life comes from, and why many are opposed to abortion and assisted suicide. You see, we do not have the right to take a life because it is not solely ours. All people belong to God. That's why he commanded us, "You shall not murder" (Exodus 20:13).

Pro-choice beliefs come from disregarding God's stake in our lives as our Creator. Human life does not belong to us alone, so we do not have the authority to end it on demand. The pro-choice movement believes it is solely the woman's right to decide, yet this ignores God's claim to the life within her. The argument states a woman has the right to do with her body whatever she chooses. But this claim falls apart when we recognize that the child she carries is not a part of her body, but another human being, whose existence is also bound to both God and the father. A woman carries out the gestation and birth process because God designed her with this ability. She does not will the child into existence—he does. Women do not have the ability to create life on their own. Life is not ours to give, so it is not ours to take.

A worldview rooted in God's truth leads to profoundly different values, which significantly affects individual and societal decisions, leading to a radically different world. Readers who believe in him know this. If you don't believe in God, sincerely seek the truth for your own spiritual well-being and conscience.

In these times, so many people don't believe in God and won't even consider the possibility of his existence. They may call themselves agnostics, atheists or realists and say, "I just don't know" or "I don't care." Yet ignoring the reality of God leads to man-made gods, which is idolatry.

The Lure of Idolatry

Let's clarify what idolatry means. When people do not know the true God, they still need a framework of reality to live by, so we must believe something in order to function in the world. As a result, we make up our own beliefs or accept moral frameworks from the surrounding culture. And whatever we hold to be right becomes our guiding light in life, like a god. But these are man-made truths and morals, absent of God.

Idols are not restricted to images carved of wood and stone and overlaid with gold and precious gems. They include a worldview that consisted of creation stories, moral codes, and life purposes for their believers. Even in ancient times, idol worship had its own theology, anthropology, knowledge, ethics and salvation.

Man-made gods of any kind are idols, including modern concepts of what is true. These are often created when a partial truth is elevated above all else and substituted for God. Though they may take the form of noble causes or deeply held beliefs within our worldview—even hidden in our subconscious—they remain false gods, shaping the decisions we make.

Ancient civilizations were not stupid. They tried to bring order to their societies by having a common, unifying set of beliefs. But of course, an idol's power is based on what people believe about it, which, back then, reflected the wisdom of the high priests and kings and their interpretations of reality and truth, rather than God's, who knows everything. In every sense, these were complete worldviews addressing the creation of man and the universe, the afterlife, morals, knowledge and theology.

Likewise, many modern idols are taking the place of God today. Science and technology study the nature of the universe apart from God and are elevated to be objective knowledge and the guiding rule for people's core beliefs. We saw previously the complete lack of moral foundation within the scientific beliefs of Darwinism and the Big Bang theory. Darwin took the observable truth of variation and claimed it to be the absolute truth of the creation of a species, absent from God. And Social Darwinism's tenet of survival of the fittest will hardly lead to a peaceful coexistence with our fellow humans.

When we deny the Creator, all we are left with is the best explanation someone can think of—a man-made truth, an idol. This also applies to the Big Bang theory. Deny God and then come up with the best explanation for the existence of the perfectly balanced and ordered universe and, by chance, the exact conditions necessary for life itself on earth in all its amazing forms.

Then there are the social sciences—fields such as psychology and sociology—that apply scientific and statistical methods to human behavior but are not "exact" in the way physics or chemistry can be. Some scholars and schools of thought argue human beings can ultimately be explained in purely physical, chemical and genetic terms—that spirit or individuality are reducible to biology. For those who take that view, the idea becomes an idol: the conviction that scientific study alone will one day give us complete knowledge of the person and the power to "fix" what is wrong.

During my undergraduate studies in biology in the 1970s, prior to the mapping of the human genome, my professors anticipated being able to modify or select genetic traits to eliminate undesirable characteristics. The disturbing ramifications of using genetics to correct what is wrong with us were shocking to me. And if they could figure out how to do this, they would have godlike abilities to know a person purely by their physical nature alone and then fix whatever is wrong with them. Of course, they would be the ones deciding what to manipulate.

In an attempt to correct what's wrong with us, there are medical protocols for some psychological conditions that treat the chemical reactions that occur in the brain. The scans of addicts can show disproportionate activity in many parts of that organ. Medication can correct these imbalances in the brain and aid its proper functioning. But that doesn't mean chemical reactions cause thoughts and feelings. Rather, they are the result of thoughts, feelings and even sensations.

The general population views the social sciences with the same regard as they do natural sciences. However, the complexity and variability of human behavior make it impossible to have the same kind of precision as the natural sciences do, which means findings in the social sciences are less definitive. If psychology were as precise as chemistry and physics, our choices and actions would be perfectly predictable, but they are not. If they were, the decisions of parole boards would be as certain as chemical reactions. While psychology does provide some insight into human behavior, it does not do so with the certainty of a chemist. Recidivism of criminals in general is very high for all races in the US.[38]

Psychology does not offer a clear understanding of what constitutes a human being in terms of mind, body or spirit. Unfortunately, this leads to Supreme Court justices (Ketanji Brown Jackson) who cannot define what a woman is.[39] Even though the social sciences should not be accepted with the same reliability as an exact science, people still believe what expert psychologists and sociologists preach.

One effect of psychology and sociology is that we now commonly view evil as a sickness instead of recognizing it for what it is. For example, pedophilia is described as a mental illness, not as wickedness. Experts will say they have misplaced sexual desire or a personality disorder. *No.* To be sexually aroused by a child is evil. To engage in any sexual act with a youth is clearly wicked, no matter what justification someone makes in their mind. The pedophile is violating an innocent's psyche, their soul, not just their body! People who do this know it is wrong, yet they still give in to their evil desires.

To be fair, the practice of psychology, especially neuropsychology, has shed real light on the role of brain chemistry in conditions such as depression, autism spectrum disorder, and schizophrenia. In many cases, medications can correct imbalances and improve both daily functioning and quality of life for the individuals affected. They can support the brain in serving the individual more effectively. But

---

[38] "Justice Department Releases Ten-Year Recidivism Study," *Prison Legal News*, March 1, 2022, charlesmastroni.com/recidivism.
[39] Caroline Downey, "Judge Jackson Refuses to Define 'Woman' during Confirmation Hearing: 'I'm Not a Biologist,'" *Yahoo! News*, March 23, 2022, charlesmastroni.com/jackson.

this does not mean that the person's invisible, spiritual self consists of chemicals and tissue alone, nor that medicine can fix everyone. Correcting chemical imbalances may enhance freedom and ability, but our core beliefs, our will, our choices, and our worldview are not dictated by brain chemistry. These belong to the spiritual dimension of life, not the material.

No doubt, some choices, such as chronic alcohol and drug use, change brain chemistry and eventually develop into a disease. Addicts are consumed by an uncontrolled desire for the abused substance and often believe they don't have a problem. However, overcoming addictions requires powerful core changes in the addict's beliefs that can eventually overcome the diseased brain chemistry. First, they need to acknowledge the truth that they are addicted. Second, they have to choose not to indulge in the substance. Then, third, they must apply their inner strength to continue making the right choice to free themselves. There is no chemical to fix this, although there are medicines that will decrease withdrawal symptoms. However, exerting the will to overcome it is what finally leads to healing.

A struggle with addiction can show two things: that an individual can be driven to live terribly by something outside themselves (for example, a chemical) and that the spiritual part of a person, their individual self, can overcome such damage. False beliefs and addictive substances can harm us, but spiritual change can defeat both.

Psychology has discovered many valuable insights, yet it shies away from claiming any objective spiritual truth. It addresses some problematic beliefs, emotions, behaviors and even brain chemistry, but it does not engage the full reality of what a human being is spiritually and morally, nor does it offer a standard definition of a human being beyond cultural norms. Without a comprehensive understanding of what it means to be human, psychology deals with people as they are and helps them function within existing societal expectations. It does not, and cannot, restore people to the true image of God.

While medicines can aid a patient, psychology does not claim to cure criminal behavior, overarching egotism, psychopathy, lust for power, greed, jealousy or any of the seven deadly sins. If an individual lives by these character traits and wants to change, then counseling may help them modify their worldview, beliefs and motivations, which can also help them spiritually. Therapy can succeed, but there is no guarantee, as there is with a chemical reaction, which yields the same result time after time. Genuine change requires an individual to alter their beliefs. Although we think of psychology and sociology as sciences, they lack the same authority regarding objective truth that we associate with the word *science*.

The same is true of the field of genetics, another developing idol in these times. Scientists have identified the specific functions of many genes, yet the exact relationship among them remain unclear. What else does a given gene cause or prevent when activated? Does one gene influence the function of another? One set of DNA in a single cell is tiny, yet it has all the instructions needed for every bodily function and for forming new cells, organs and tissues. For such a small amount of material with so much responsibility, each gene must have more than one function, especially in its interactions with other genes.

Scientists are pursuing gene editing to cure diseases. However, medicines that alter genes can carry many unintended consequences. Our spirits are inseparably integrated with our bodies, for when they are separated, we die. Still, geneticists don't know whether, or how, our spiritual self is connected to our genetic makeup.

Some scientists and philosophers take a fully materialist view, denying that humankind has a soul. To them, we are nothing more than physicochemical reactions, wholly determined by our genetics. We have no soul, no will, no individuality, no real choice—everything we are and do is simply the inevitable result of our genetic code and chemistry.

As Anthony Cashmore, a New Zealand biochemist and molecular biologist, puts it:

> Finally, I would like to make the following point: in the introductory chapter of many undergraduate texts dealing with biology or biochemistry, it is common to stress (as I have in this article) that biological systems obey the laws of chemistry and physics; as living systems we are nothing more than a bag of chemicals … a belief in free will is nothing less than a continuing belief in vitalism—a concept that we like to think we discarded well over 100 years ago![40]

Admittedly, the majority of scientists and philosophers don't take this view. However, some claim our emotional life exists solely as a product of chemical and physical brain activity. According to this belief, romantic love, parental love, and the bonds of family and friendship are not genuine emotions but merely physicochemical processes.

Materialists believe your genetics and chemistry fully determine your decisions and that there is no such thing as spirituality. Even choices themselves are viewed as the product of physicochemical processes, not your will, individuality or effort. By this reasoning, any moral effort you make to do what is right or to be a good person is negated, reducing a human being to "just a bag of chemicals."

The logical conclusion of materialism is that people have no choice or freedom because they are not truly individuals. Human beings are reduced to chemical reactions. There is no real "you" or "me" apart from our physical bodies. This leads to the inevitable

---

[40] Anthony R. Cashmore, "The Lucretian swerve: The biological basis of human behavior and the criminal justice system," *Proceedings of the National Academy of Sciences of the United States of America* 107, no. 10 (March 9, 2010):4499–4504. doi.org/10.1073/pnas.0915161107.

belief that when we die, we simply cease to exist. In the TAKES worldview model, this is the materialist's view of salvation, which sounds to me like no salvation at all.

Ultimately, a materialist view of humanity concludes that there is no such thing as individual responsibility, will and choice. In other words, there are no evil people, but only "bad" chemistry and genes, and there are no noble people, only "good" chemistry and genes. Where does one find meaning in such a belief system? I see none. This view implies we are all stuck being as we are, unable to change or improve. There is no image of God in us, only an image of our genes.

What will this lead to if this materialistic trend is followed as truth? It could result in a government-sponsored group of scientists genetically breeding and modifying the human race, based only on their morality. Who has this wisdom? Humankind and governments have not demonstrated it, nor have scientists, for none of them are morally superior to God.

This bleak scenario is the stuff of futuristic novels, such as *Brave New World, 1984, Fahrenheit 451,* and *A Clockwork Orange.* The writers of these books followed the science and philosophy of post-Christian times to its natural conclusion. They merely rolled down the tracks where godless trains of thought led. Without God, who has the objective wisdom of what is good and evil, there is no hope for humanity.

Of course, science, medicine and psychology have done much good as well. No one can deny that, especially in the area of medicine. But when these fields take the position that they are the final and only objective source of truth, they become idols. They are claiming objective knowledge when they don't know everything. They are not omniscient or all-wise, but God is.

More and more psychology has gone in this materialistic direction. What is the scientific solution to depression? Prescriptions. What is the scientific solution to ADHD? Prescriptions. Yes, chemical imbalances cause depression, ADHD, schizophrenia and other mental health issues, and science has found treatments. That is helpful. It's not that science knows nothing, but some of its adherents take this knowledge and extrapolate it to encompass all human maladies.

Although some of these disorders can be treated with medicine, evil at its core is a spiritual problem, not merely a chemical one. Violent behavior is often labeled as antisocial personality disorder. *Disorder* is a sanitized word used to describe the behavior of someone who attacks others, lies, cheats or disregards the rights of those around them. In psychology, this dispassionate language is meant to analyze antisocial behavior in a "scientific" and rational way. Psychologists may understand the technical meaning behind these words, but to the general public, this language often distorts reality. It creates the impression that such behavior is simply a sickness, when in truth it is evil in action.

Murderers and child molesters are commonly described as "sick" people, when in fact they are driven by evil desires. This is one of the subtle yet powerful effects psychology has had on our culture. A more accurate description for someone with antisocial personality disorder would be liar, cheater, abuser, murderer or simply sinner. These plain words carry emotional weight. They touch the conscience and can move a person toward repentance and change. Ultimately, an antisocial person does not merely have a "disorder." They have deep moral and spiritual problems. Unless their inmost self is transformed, their evil acts will persist.

The choice of terminology used by a psychologist creates the impression of scientific precision—that they know exactly what motivates a person. But there is no such certainty. It also suggests psychotherapy can solve these spiritual problems of the psyche for personality disorders, and that genetics may play a role in these conditions.[41]

---

[41] "Personality Disorders," Cleveland Clinic, reviewed April 16, 2022, charlesmastroni.com/personalitydisorders.

Psychiatrists may conduct brain scans, but antisocial behavior is ultimately a spiritual problem, not a physical one. The core issue is self-centeredness. People with this pattern of behavior are neither God-centered nor other-centered. They simply indulge their desires. Counseling and traditional psychotherapy, which examine a person's thoughts, attitudes and behaviors, can address a spiritual problem more effectively than medications alone. The basic spiritual problem is that the person doesn't care that they are accountable to God or their fellow humans, or that they are to "do to others as you would have them do to you," as Jesus taught (Luke 6:31 NIV).

Extreme academics who are materialists assume evil has a chemical cause, and they believe they will someday find it. If they can just identify the right genes to alter or eliminate or medications to administer, we can perfect humanity. This view is easily incorporated into diagnoses and treatments. How many prescriptions are written purely to see if they will work? It is impossible to tell.

However, concerns have been raised that ADHD has been overdiagnosed and that the medication used to treat it has been overprescribed.[42] Millions of children worldwide have been prescribed amphetamines, which harms many of them. Children's brains are still developing until their early twenties.[43] How can the widespread practice of giving low-dose speed to so many children be beneficial without long-term consequences?

And then we have the materialist influence of genetics leading to designer babies. Potential parents intentionally select eggs and

---

[42] Luise Kazda, Katy Bell, Rae Thomas, Kevin McGeechan, Rebecca Sims, and Alexandra Barratt, "Overdiagnosis of Attention-Deficit/Hyperactivity Disorder in Children and Adolescents: A Systematic Scoping Review," *JAMA Network Open* 4, no. 4 (April 12, 2021): e215335, doi.org/10.1001/jamanetworkopen.2021.5335.

[43] Staff, "How the Brain Develops," *Psychology Today*, accessed January 8, 2026, charlesmastroni.com/braindevelopment.

sperm donated from people with certain desirable traits related to intelligence, hair color, eye color, size and athletic ability, assuming the child will inherit most or all of the chosen qualities. This is more like animal husbandry, and implanting the fertilized eggs is a lot less fun than sexual intercourse.

Psychology has had a tremendous influence on our culture. A small percentage of individuals in the world may have true gender dysphoria. However, educators, school psychologists, and school boards are now teaching this as a real possibility to children, who are very impressionable and suggestible. They have named this condition and then applied it to students as if it could be true for every child. The truth is that throughout human history and in the animal kingdom, there are two sexes, and neither people nor any higher animals physically switch between genders without surgery. Even if you believe in evolution, humanity developed from nature into two physical sexes that are fixed and unchanging to ensure the continuation of the human race, which should be important to us all.

Certainly, some people have felt since an early age that they are the opposite gender than their physical body suggests and may identify themselves that way. These individuals should not be bullied, attacked or persecuted. Please do not conclude that I hate them or that most people do. We may feel surprised, yes. But hate? No. People experiencing gender dysphoria should be treated with the same consideration as anyone else. But public schools are hardly qualified to determine whether children have it.

What I object to is the current progressive agenda that insists everyone must believe gender is fluid and accept someone as a biologically natural woman or man simply because they identify as one. This has led to physical males competing against physical females based on self-identification alone. The woke cancel culture demands the world adopt this redefinition of *woman* and *man*, requiring us to abandon our fundamental belief of what a man or a woman is and replace it with their version of the truth. Either you accept it, or you will be canceled and treated with contempt. At best, they condescendingly say you must be reeducated to embrace the science of modern psychology, suspending your understanding of truth in favor of theirs.

There is certainly more to being a man than the ability to impregnate a woman, and more to being a woman than the ability to bear children. However, this does not change the reality that we are physical beings, and part of being a biologically complete male is the ability to impregnate a female, while part of being a biologically complete female is the ability to bear children. The truth is, this is how nature works—otherwise, the human race would not have lasted this long.

We are physical and spiritual beings with a body and a psyche. The so-called new truth of fluctuating gender identity does not eliminate the natural truth humanity has known and believed in all cultures since the beginning of time. It is wrong to hate people with gender identity issues. I do strongly object, however, to psychology and progressive culture demanding we redefine a man and a woman according to their liking, not God's created order.

Academics often build careers by finding exceptions to a rule, then arguing the rule itself is no longer valid. They write books and papers claiming we all must change our understanding and accept everything they present as new truth. Transgender theory emerged around 1975.[44] Are we now supposed to question the basic truths of nature simply because academics say so? The existence of exceptions does not disprove the rule. For example, just because some people commit murder does not mean murder is morally acceptable or legally permissible. In the same way, just because a few individuals do not conform to typical male or female biological patterns, this does not mean there are multiple or fluid

---

[44] Jack Turban, "The Disturbing History of Research into Transgender Identity," *Scientific American*, October 23, 2020, doi.org/10.1038/scientificamericanmind0121-28.

genders. The basic rule remains: the vast majority of males and females fall into the standard biological categories.

Many school boards are requiring teachers to ask students questions to consider whether they are the "wrong" sex, especially if they act outside traditional gender norms. But are children—or even teachers—truly qualified to make such a determination? The answer is no. Children lack the mental and emotional maturity to make fully informed decisions about permanent, life-altering medical interventions. In fact, many choices are rightly and legally prohibited to them. For example, in the US, children under eighteen cannot even legally enter contracts or purchase cigarettes. In most states, those under sixteen cannot drive or give legal consent to sexual activity under statutory rape laws. These restrictions exist to protect children because they are not developmentally equipped to weigh the long-term consequences of their actions and can be unduly influenced by adults.[45] Why are authorities allowing and even suggesting children make decisions about altering their bodies, including hormone treatments and surgeries, well before they are mature enough to understand the consequences? Evil hides behind good intentions, cloaking itself in appealing names like "gender-affirming care."

By nature, our genders differ physically and psychologically. Boys and girls gravitate toward different activities and interests from a very early age—before nine months old when socialization starts to shape them.[46] This does not mean the two genders are unequal. Christianity teaches they are different but equal, for both are made in the image of God. Today, our lives are so removed from the natural world that we have lost touch with basic instinctive knowledge that even animals know. For proof of this,

---

[45] Lindsay Tanner, "Trans kids' treatment can start younger, new guidelines say," *Associated Press News*, June 15, 2022, charlesmastroni.com/transkids.
[46] NeuroLaunch editorial team, "Boy and Girl Behavior Differences: Nature, Nurture, and Societal Influences," *NeuroLaunch*, September 22, 2024, charlesmastroni.com/childbehavior.

just observe animals in heat. They know the difference between males and females. Only in the godless heights of the ivory towers of academia, far removed from real life, could ignoring these differences be acceptable or treated as fundamental truth.

Children are very suggestible and impressionable, especially when interacting with authority figures. This is why it is considered morally wrong for teachers to engage in sexual activity with their students. Isn't it even more egregious to probe a child about their gender and suggest they alter it? In the 1970s, society largely accepted sex education in our schools, which replaced the traditional birds-and-the-bees talk that was a parent's responsibility. The schools claimed they were better-equipped and convinced parents they could do a superior job.

What have we progressed to now? In many schools, transgender theory is presented to children as a real possibility. This has led, in some cases, to hormone treatments and surgeries on prepubescents. It is neither wise nor morally right to physically alter an individual before they possess the wisdom and emotional maturity to decide for themselves, no matter how many tests or explanations are given. If this is not the stuff of a *Brave New World*, I don't know what is.

Changing genders is a false promise. For over 99.8 percent of the population, one's sex at birth is biologically fixed as male or female, with very rare genetic anomalies.[47] Surgeries and hormone treatments may create the appearance of the opposite gender, but they cannot actually become a different sex, no matter what they may think and feel internally. Telling children that their sex can be changed is a lie—only the appearance of gender is able to be altered. Gender is both physical and psychological. This historic, fundamental truth about gender,

---

[47] Nasir A. M. Al-Jurayyan, "Disorders of Sex Development (DSD): A More Than Three Decades of Experience at a Major Teaching Hospital," *International Journal of Clinical Endocrinology and Metabolism* 10, no. 1 (2024): 014–017, doi.org/10.17352/ijcem.000061.

reflected in books, love stories, comedies, plays and movies, is right, even if some psychologists disagree.

This objective truth of nature enables life to reproduce "according to its kind," as stated in Genesis. Male and female, men and women, are the natural order. However, a psychological diagnosis of gender dysphoria can lead to permanent, life-changing interventions that result in irreversible infertility. Some psychologists insist this action is right, true, wise and good for their patients. Instinct, common sense, and intuition say it's not. This is a clear example of authorities overstepping, playing God, and defying basic truth. Suggesting to children that they may not really be a boy or a girl, simply because a very few feel otherwise, is harmful and confusing. That this takes place within school systems is modern idolatry.

Progressives worship their idols of psychological science and medical technology, supported by government power and school boards. And they are sacrificing our children to their beliefs and worldviews, often with tragic consequences. For example, some may decide to pursue gender surgery, believing it will make them happy, but the procedure does nothing to address any underlying psychological conditions (such as depression, childhood trauma, and prior suicidal attempts) that may have contributed to the desire for the surgery in the first place. Yet, when coexisting psychiatric disorders are appropriately treated, feelings of gender discomfort have been shown to lessen or resolve.[48] Instead, irreversible, life-changing surgery is offered under the banner of the modern idols of inclusion: love, kindness, fairness, gender-affirming care, equity, nonjudgmentalism, acceptance, understanding, compassion, civil rights, and whatever other progressive, self-congratulatory principles they champion. And anyone who disagrees, relying on

---

[48] Moises H. Serrano, Paul B. Thompson, and Michael J. Berry, "Ethical Issues in Genetic Testing and Genetic Counseling," *Journal of Genetic Counseling* 18, no. 3 (June 2009): 231–237, doi.org/10.1177/10398562241276978.

common sense, experience and observation, is dismissed as an unevolved Cro-Magnon, troglodyte, transphobic, religious nut.

What makes a man or woman is plain to see.
It's been obvious for centuries.

Academics now say this is a lie.
They say don't believe what's in front of your eyes.

The woke now demand you must awaken.
All art of the past must be mistaken.

Believe what we tell you, not what you see.
You must listen to all the PhDs.

Justice Jackson can't tell who's a she.
This has not been a problem for me.

I chased them all when I was twenty-three!

CHAPTER 7

Foundations of Progressivism

Godless progressivism has developed a comprehensive worldview that seeks to replace traditional religious belief systems, offering its own version of "truth" in every area of TAKES, except in providing a clear moral framework. To its adherents, progressivism functions as a religion in all but name.

I was seventy years old when I wrote this book. Born in the mid-1950s, I have lived through the march of these "new truths" into the Western world, beginning with the cultural revolution of the 1960s. I watched as God was systematically removed from our public schools and societal discourse under the banner of an overzealous separation of church and state. These days, nothing related to Christianity can be connected with any government activity. Even long-standing religious symbols have been stripped from public buildings and monuments across the country.

I have also witnessed the profound shift from individual responsibility to group responsibility. How many times have you heard the maxim "we are all at fault" or "the system failed us" when there is yet another school shooting? The wish and assumption of this sentiment is that society (namely schools, teachers, other students, lawmakers or psychologists) should have somehow prevented it. This shift toward corporate responsibility for individual actions is evidenced by lawsuits against fast-food chains for causing obesity[49] and in laws that hold a restaurant or party host responsible if someone drives drunk after leaving their premises. In this way of thinking, others are made responsible for an individual's actions.

Finally, I have observed that our Western culture firmly believes we are "evolved" compared to previous generations. Yet the truth is simpler: technology has advanced and expert theories abound, but human nature has not changed.

The false foundations of most of progressivism and its panorama of idols start with multiple assumptions:

1. **There is no God.** This belief is supported by the Big Bang theory, Darwinism and post-Christian existential philosophy. According to this view, the human race is evolving entirely on its own. Evolution is seen as the nature of the universe, and everything develops by accident and chance.

   Note: It is no accident that these two origin theories directly contradict the very first sentence in the Bible, "In the beginning, God created the heavens and the earth" (Genesis 1:1). Please consider this, especially if you doubt there is spiritual warfare in the world. Belief in these two theories has supplanted the reality of God or a need for him in many people's minds, hearts and souls.

2. **Science and experts—not tradition, common sense, your instincts, or religion—are the final arbiters of truth.** "Believe the science," as we heard so often during the COVID pandemic. Yet, as time has shown, scientists sometimes gave inaccurate or contradictory advice, and only one set of voices was amplified while others were silenced. Experts often disagree on any given topic. So, despite how

---

[49] Caesar Barber, "Obese Man Sues Fast-Food Chains," *ABC News,* July 25, 2002, charlesmastroni.com/obesitylawsuit.

strongly this belief has taken hold in Western culture, can science truly be the ultimate determiner of truth?

3. **There is only the natural world.** Anything supernatural is dismissed as something the human mind cannot yet explain, but eventually will. There is no proof of spirit or spiritual reality because these have not been verified by science. According to this view, your inner life is just brain chemistry, and in time, medicine will be able to fix everything. Maybe not now, but eventually.

4. **All human beings are basically good.** Evil, it is said, arises only from bad circumstances. The individual is merely a product of their environment. This half-truth, emphasized by the social sciences, is the "nurture" side of the equation. From it flows political movements, such as socialism, and practices, like social engineering, in an attempt to make a better world. It also concludes that criminals aren't responsible for their crimes because they are the victims of society.

5. **Since there is no need for God, there is no need to judge evil.** After all, we are simply products of our environment. If we can control the environment, then we can eradicate negative behaviors. In this worldview, all truth is relative, so evil is just a myth. We are "evolving past" that. (Here, I use the word we a bit sarcastically.)

6. **Governments should take control of all social constructs,** including families and education, to prevent negative environments. After all, if poor behaviors result from the environment, then regulating it should prevent them. How often do we hear the refrain "society has failed us"? And of course, the implied solution is for the government to dominate all aspects of life.

7. **Science, technology and human wisdom can solve all our problems.** If humanity can cooperate, take control, and engineer the right environment, we will succeed in building some version of utopia, nirvana or heaven on earth. And if we fail, artificial intelligence (AI) is waiting in the wings to figure everything out for us. No man-made gods here. (Again, this is sarcasm.)

I have to ask… What reading of history supports these assumptions of progressivism? Why do many in our culture believe these ideas when so much of our past consists of wars, persecution and the conquest of nations? There has always been murder, rape, adultery, theft and the lust for power, conquest and adulation. Human beings have a dark side that progressivism ignores by assuming its idol is right and good. To disagree is to be viewed as an unevolved caveman who should be canceled or reeducated. However, we are a composite of good and bad and tend to cooperate with those we identify with, leaving us suspicious of those with whom we disagree.

Every ideological idol that has tried to create heaven on earth has ultimately turned violent or oppressive to those who oppose it, including progressivism and cancel culture. Communism and its cousin, socialism, also demonstrate this pattern: the former through overt oppression and violence, the latter through regulations, bureaucracies, fines, taxes and a government that grants or withholds individual rights at its discretion. Under social democracy, a system that blends democratic governance with socialist economic and social policies, the state can remove any right it decides to, like the presence of God in government, for whatever it determines is the common good.

When corrupted, even institutionalized religions have become violent, despite the peaceful intentions of their founders. Social movements, like the hippies, and religious movements, like the Puritans, all failed to establish lasting utopias. If you are an old hippie, you may fondly remember Woodstock as a utopia, but it only lasted for a few days.

For millennia, the common sense, intuitive and instinctive beliefs of humanity have been rooted in the knowledge that the divine created the universe and established morality and natural order. People knew that a supernatural aspect of reality had been part of the history of humankind. We see this reflected in classic literature, religions and philosophies. In contrast, science's two main origin theories, along with the existential philosophy they support, provide a framework that allows people to ignore, discount and dismiss the existence of the supernatural.

No ideology of human origin has succeeded in creating heaven on earth because we have a dark, evil side to our nature. Followers of such utopian idols self-righteously assume they have overcome that flaw when they have not. Zealous adherents of progressivism won't entertain the notion that they might be wrong! They are certain their beliefs are the objective truth, even if they don't believe in objective truth. All too frequently this leads not to debate but to attempts to cancel, silence or marginalize those who disagree, and sometimes even to murder them.

Evil often disguises itself as something good or appealing, both in individuals and across cultures. Idols, in the form of ideologies, often sound appealing and plausible, but in the long run, they fail because they mimic truth without being true. That's how evil first sold itself to humanity. The serpent told Adam and Eve that disobeying God would be good for them, promising they would become like God and gain wisdom. They believed this lie, and we continue to do so, in part, if not in full, which is all that is needed for evil to succeed.

> But the serpent said to the woman, "You will not
> surely die. For God knows that when you eat of it
> your eyes will be opened, and you will be like God,
> knowing good and evil." So when the woman saw
> that the tree was good for food, and that it was
> a delight to the eyes, and that the tree was to be

> desired to make one wise, she took of its fruit and
> ate, and she also gave some to her husband who
> was with her, and he ate (Genesis 3:4–6).

Adam and Eve believed they were getting something good when they ignored God's warning. They thought they were making the right decision by taking the knowledge of evil into themselves. Blatant evil is too easy to recognize, so it cloaks itself in deception. The same is true of man-made ideologies. They may sound good, but they are not.

Communism sold itself to the poor as freedom from oppression, but when it gained control, it became severely oppressive. So what was the real motivation behind it: justice or power?

We are no different today. Some blatantly revel in wrongdoing, but very few consciously choose what they know to be evil, except for psychopaths. (By the way, psychology classifies psychopathy as a personality disorder.) Overwhelmingly, most people indulging in evil justify it as good in some way.

Ted Kaczynski, the Unabomber, believed he was doing good when he resisted the military-industrial complex and the mechanization of society. Timothy McVeigh justified the Oklahoma City bombing as retaliation for government oppression at Waco. In the 1960s, revolutionaries like the Weathermen bombed government buildings, claiming to fight US imperialism and war. Abortion clinic bombers defend their actions as protecting unborn children. The Spanish Inquisition, though aimed at rooting out heresy, often resorted to torture to force confessions, believing this served God's cause. Islamic terrorists call America the "Great Satan" and Israel the "Little Satan," framing violence as holy war. In the USSR, the Communist Party punished dissenters by sending them to gulags or declaring them insane, insisting such cruelty preserved the party's "truth." Any citizens who publicly disagreed with the party were declared insane and put in prisons for reeducation.[50] And social engineers of the present day think they are doing good by reshaping society according to their idols.

When people blindly adhere to an ideology, the evil within human nature eventually reveals itself, masked by the banner of righteousness. Cancel culture is a definite step in that direction since its proponents believe its truth must be the only truth. These present-day idol worshippers believe they are doing good; therefore, anyone opposed to them needs to be silenced, canceled or killed.

On a national or cultural scale, evil still hides behind a good cause to convince the general population that it is right and must be obeyed. Nazi Germany, Joseph Stalin's USSR, Chairman Mao's China, and many other dictators provide stark examples of this. Under their rule, the promised utopia often became a hell on earth, not the heaven they promised. Communism, from its intellectual founders Karl Marx and Friedrich Engels, is explicitly atheist and anti-religion, denying the existence of God. The commonly repeated phrase "Religion is the opium of the people"[51] comes right from Marx.

The pattern is clear. Find a cause that convinces people to support it, gaining power through their belief and obedience. When enough power is attained, use it to eliminate anyone or anything that does not comply with the cause. It doesn't matter whether the obedience is willing or coerced. Once in power, control the education of people and the media to indoctrinate the population into its supposed truth and persecute any dissent to destroy opposition.

In communist regimes, those in control used propaganda to ensure people believed them and willingly obeyed, while others

---

[50] Stuart Roberts, "State of Madness: Psychiatry, Literature, and Dissent After Stalin," *University of Cambridge,* accessed January 8, 2026, charlesmastroni. com/communistdissent.

[51] David R. Papke, "Karl Marx on Religion," *Faculty Blog, Marquette University Law School,* January 20, 2015, charlesmastroni.com/marxonreligion.

obeyed out of fear of being punished. The Communist Party hid its actions behind the promise of a worker's paradise and shared wealth. Leaders like Vladimir Lenin, Leon Trotsky and Joseph Stalin outlawed opposing political parties by killing or imprisoning its members, controlled all news and cultural output, and took over the education of children, instilling the party's version of truth, history and worldview. (In other words, they systematically brainwashed the population.) But this had a damaging effect on the spirit of their people.

Hitler and the Nazi Party in Germany hid behind the claim that they wanted to restore national pride and create a superior race. They followed the same formula, seizing control of the culture and media, outlawing political opposition, and indoctrinating the youth through the Hitlerjugend (Hitler Youth) program. Nazi ideology effectively replaced religion, taking over churches and demanding allegiance to the Führer instead of God. Schools, movies, radio and museums all promoted the Nazi Party's worldview and its distorted understanding of truth, including a rewritten history that emphasized the superiority of the Aryan race.

Chairman Mao implemented atheistic communism in much the same way: taking over education, burning books, and annihilating any political opponents or dissension. The government indoctrinated the youth and purged the nation of the older generations who did not accept Mao as absolutely right and worthy of obedience and loyalty.

These ideologies eliminated all dissent—their version of cancel culture on a grand scale. Proponents viewed unity as complete conformity to their truth and rejected free thought and free speech, permitting no God or other authority but themselves.

Many of the progressive idols listed above use most or all of the same methods of hiding evil behind an appearance of good. Their propaganda is called "controlling the narrative." If you do not fully accept the claims of climate activists (that all modern life should be stripped of fossil fuels or humanity will die), you are labeled an insane "climate denier." According to these progressive zealots, there is no room for debate—dissenters must be silenced.

The same holds true for diversity, equity and inclusion (DEI) or critical race theory (CRT). If you don't believe in these frameworks, you are often branded a racist and a horrible human being. Therefore, you must lose your job. CRT views the history of Western civilization completely through the lens of racism, so of course, that is all it finds in its worldview. DEI and CRT initiatives have been implemented in many governments, schools and corporations around the world—though in recent years, there has been growing backlash and efforts to roll them back. However, proponents of these initiatives to socially engineer our world will not cease any time soon.

If you don't agree with the transgender movement, you are often hated and labeled as dangerous, a transphobe, and a horrible human being. Refuse to use the right pronouns, and you risk being fired or severely punished. Insist that marriage is between a man and a woman, and you're branded a homophobe, even though that definition has been the norm throughout human history until recently.

Many in the West today follow new idols that shape their values and policies. The idol of science drives the climate activists, even though history has shown that many dire predictions fail to materialize. Social justice has spawned idols like DEI, same-sex marriage, and the transgender movement. And the psychological sciences, supported by social justice, gave birth to the idol of the LGBTQIA+ movement.

DEI and the woke police are the priesthood of the latest attack on truth. Yet they are only the most recent expression of a trend that began long before. Since the 1960s, many belief systems have risen in popularity and become culturally accepted. That decade marked a dramatic shift in our nation's moral foundations. The popular attitude back then was: "Don't lay your moral trip on me, man." Since then, progressive idol worshippers have been laying their moral trip on everyone else and enshrining their idols into law whenever they can.

People claiming to be nonjudgmental have imposed a constant stream of judgments on traditional values. A common accusation against religious people is that they are overly critical. But they are no more so than anyone else. The progressive DEI and woke crowd enforces its views just as forcefully and often more aggressively. They simply have a different set of beliefs they want to impose on the rest of society. To them, I say, "Don't lay your moral trip on me either."

This progressive worldview purports to do good and be right, according to the idols they worship and obey. It enjoys strong backing from universities, school boards, and much of the Western political establishment. Over the past decades, God has been systematically removed from public life in the US, beginning with decisions like the elimination of prayer in schools in 1962. Laws are increasingly used to punish those who disagree with these progressive idols. Yet money remains the oldest and perhaps most powerful idol of all, giving the wealthy and well-connected immense power over public policy and culture.

The Bias of Science

When it comes to climate change, scientists use models to measure environmental variations and predict future effects. But are they reliable? Not according to the Capital Research Center:

> Much of the fear of global warming, now called climate change, stems from long-term projections that use complex climate models. These are correctly called projections, not predictions, because none of the models has undergone the rigorous scientific testing required for verification and validation. Consequently, the models and their

> results are speculative. If a climate model had been verified and validated, that would be the only model needed. As it is, we have multiple models producing a wide variety of projections. A critical issue in global warming/climate change science is the reliability of the models and the evidence substantiating their use.[52]

Many scientists still assume their models provide enough accurate data and they understand enough weather patterns to make dire predictions. These lead to demands for drastic changes in everyone's life.

Some scientists are well-intentioned in their efforts to warn the world based on what they have determined is the truth. They believe their research is sound and want us to as well, but their models are fallible because their developers aren't omniscient. Other scientists may be intentionally deceitful. They want funding for their work and to gain prestige by breaking new ground. Financial backing often comes from political sources and wealthy benefactors, who want even more power and influence. And since big changes provide opportunities for power, they position themselves to affect government policies to achieve their own goals.

Scientists are not anymore angelic than the rest of humanity. Researchers who receive grants and other funding from these sources will continue to do so as long as the results of their studies are beneficial to their backers. Some scientists will perform diligent ethical research and impartially report the results. Others will construct their studies to achieve conclusions that suit their benefactor's goals since continued funding will be dependent on the conclusions they come to.

---

[52] Kenneth Happala, "A Short History of Global Warming Fears," *ClimateDollars.org*, accessed January 8, 2026. charlesmastroni.com/globalwarmingfears.

> Not all of this government funding goes to advocacy of climate alarmism, of course. But it would be hard for the federal government to spend billions of dollars a year on a controversial topic, with every penny of the spending based on the presumption that global warming is a serious crisis worthy of billions of tax dollars, and not have those billions make a powerful impression on the public. The persons in the public who would be most powerfully affected would be those hoping to obtain grants for their research, or tax subsidies for their businesses, or otherwise seeking to benefit from going along with the presumption that a crisis exists. Tens of billions of dollars are not exactly a small incentive.[53]

Even if we presume that politicians, the wealthy, the powerful, and scientists are all acting with good intentions, the old saying still holds true: the road to hell is paved with good intentions. And if some of these believers in the idol of climate change have bad intentions, that road only gets shorter.

Science will always be limited in its knowledge because it is not God. Whether people are accurate or mistaken, well- or ill-intentioned about climate change, it is unwise to blindly accept doomsday predictions that will grant governments the power to control our lives completely and take our freedom. Yet much of the world is now convinced by this idol that life will end unless we conform, and many are willing to do so out of fear.

---

[53] Kenneth Haapala, "U.S. Government Funding of Climate Change," *ClimateDollars.org*, accessed January 9, 2026. charlesmastroni.com/climatechangefunding.

The Cost of Man-Made Ideologies

You might think you are immune to these cornerstones of progressivism, but when they gain influence and power, it becomes all too easy to follow along, whether their direction is right or wrong, good or evil. In Western culture, science itself has become an unquestioned authority we often obey without hesitation.

This tendency was demonstrated in the famous Milgram experiment.[54] In 1963, psychologist Stanley Milgram conducted a study at Yale University to explore why people obey authority figures, inspired by questions about German obedience during World War II. Male volunteers were told they were participating in a study on learning and memory. Each was assigned the role of "teacher" and instructed to administer increasingly strong electric shocks to a "learner" (an actor) whenever the learner gave a wrong answer.

Despite hearing apparent distress from the learner, most participants continued giving shocks when urged by the experimenter. About two-thirds went all the way to the highest voltage level of 450 volts, while all the participants continued up to at least 300 volts.

Milgram concluded that ordinary people will often obey authority figures, even to the point of killing—regardless of whether doing so conflicts with their personal conscience or causes harm to others.

I know we like to think we wouldn't obey the historical evil leaders of the world (such as Adolf Hitler, Joseph Stalin, Chairman Mao, or Saddam Hussein), but Milgram's findings indicate otherwise. As long as we believe we are obeying the authorities, the party line, the controlled narrative, or the consensus, we will easily be led to do evil or harmful actions.

---

[54] Saul McLeod, "The Milgram Shock Experiment," *College Reading and Writing*, Lumen Learning, accessed January 9, 2026. charlesmastroni.com/milgram.

The Milgram experiment echoes the refrain of those who obeyed their Nazi leaders as they carried out the genocide of over six million Jews (and an estimated five to eleven million Romani people, disabled citizens, Polish and Soviet civilians, political prisoners, and others deemed "undesirable") and justified going to war with the rest of the world. "I was just following orders."

The Bible explains what happens with man-made ideologies when people try to make heaven for themselves without God. In Genesis, we learn about the Tower of Babel, which describes humanity's efforts to achieve heaven on its own terms. The wisdom in this scripture accurately describes all man-made idols, including causes and gods.

Here is a little context and background for this story. In the previous chapters of Genesis, before the Tower of Babel, we learn about Noah and the flood. People had become so evil that God could not tolerate humanity. This pained God:

> The Lord saw how great the wickedness of the human race had become on the earth, and that every inclination of the thoughts of the human heart was only evil all the time. The Lord regretted that he had made human beings on the earth, and his heart was deeply troubled. So the Lord said, "I will wipe from the face of the earth the human race I have created" (Genesis 6:5–7 NIV).

In this biblical story, God flooded the world, yet he rescued Noah and his family and preserved the animal kingdom for a new start. God then told them to go forth, multiply and fill the earth; the same thing he told Adam and Eve, because that was his command for humankind. "Then God blessed Noah and his sons, saying to them, 'Be fruitful and increase in number and fill the earth'" (Genesis 9:1 NIV). Yet even with this mandate from God and the punishment he justly executed in the flood, humanity still did not listen to or seek him. Instead, they decided to build their own tower to heaven.

Now, the oral traditions of many ancient societies all had some version of a flood story. The descendants of Noah—the cultures that developed after the restart—knew of the great flood. Yet they still relied solely on their idea of what was good. The Tower of Babel was humanity's response as they asserted their self-sufficiency and pride, thinking that they didn't need God. This is the lesson from the Tower of Babel:

> Now the whole world had one language and a common speech. As people moved eastward, they found a plain in Shinar and settled there.
>
> They said to each other, "Come, let's make bricks and bake them thoroughly." They used brick instead of stone, and tar for mortar. Then they said, "Come, let us build ourselves a city, with a tower that reaches to the heavens, so that we may make a name for ourselves; otherwise we will be scattered over the face of the whole earth."
>
> But the Lord came down to see the city and the tower the people were building. The Lord said, "If as one people speaking the same language they have begun to do this, then nothing they plan to do will be impossible for them. Come, let us go down and confuse their language so they will not understand each other."
>
> So the Lord scattered them from there over all the earth, and they stopped building the city. That is why it was called Babel—because there the Lord confused the language of the whole world. From

> there the Lord scattered them over the face of the
> whole earth (Genesis 11:1–9 NIV).

The purpose of the tower itself was to give meaning to peoples' lives, and it was their attempt to get to heaven without God.

God created stone, used as a witness of truth in scripture. It was always used for altars and was not to be shaped by man's tools. Jesus is even described as the cornerstone of the church (Ephesians 2:20–22). Bricks, however, are a symbol of man-made truths—human attempts to construct meaning apart from God.

In some translations, the word *tar* is rendered as *slime*. Under the heat of the sun, tar softens and slides, a fitting image for the instability of human efforts without God. At the Tower of Babel, the people refused to acknowledge him and defied his command to fill the earth despite knowing he had recently flooded the world in an act of judgment against humanity's corruption and rebellion.

Was God being mean? No, he was exercising his divine prerogative to fulfill one of his instructions for humanity—to fill the earth. God's will, his truth, is what must be obeyed, not our limited understanding of what seems good to us. Seeing the rampant evil that persisted in human hearts, he intervened once again. He knew our attempts to create heaven on earth without him would always lead to ruin, so by scattering the people, he ensured his plan for humanity would be carried out.

God knows that eventually, our ideologies, knowledge and good intentions always miss the mark. He sees the whole objective truth. We do not. Therefore, every human attempt to build a utopian society or a tower to heaven ultimately leads to evil and disaster. If you doubt this, let's look at history's pattern. Whenever a movement or leader gains enough economic, political and military power, the result is the same: force, oppression and totalitarian rule. Kings, pharaohs, sultans, dictators, revolutionary movements like communism, emperors like in Rome and China, and even the social engineers of our own times—all have used some combination of fear, death, torture, starvation, oppression, laws, fines and taxes to dominate those they control. Power always corrupts. God knows this better than any historian or philosopher. He has given us wisdom and truth in the Bible, and we are foolish to reject it.

The Pantheon of Modern Idols

Academics originated this current progressivism in our universities based on their own reasoning and intelligence. Since they are highly educated, many see themselves as the most evolved among us. Confident in their own wisdom, they spawned this amorphous combination of idols, all under the banner of "progress." These include movements such as LGBTQIA+ advocacy, pro-science, environmentalism and anti-religion philosophies, opposition to Creationism, anti-capitalism, feminism, hostility toward marriage and masculinity, and the fixation on systemic racism. They worship their theories and causes as idols—championing them in the name of goodness, individual rights, civil rights, progress, and human evolution. In turn, they produce students who are faithful to the same idols.

We touched earlier on the gender-fluid idolatry of current psychology. There is no clearer example of experts and authorities running amok than their advocacy for transgender athletes. Why do so many organizations accept this? Full-grown men who were born male and now have adult male bodies are competing against women. And sports authorities have allowed this.[55] They even claim that to do otherwise is discrimination from a social justice perspective. Men simply decide to identify as female. They have no rare genetic physical anomalies, yet they believe they are women and therefore argue they should be allowed to compete against

---

[55] Sonia Twigg, "Are There Any Transgender Athletes Competing at the 2024 Olympics?," *The Independent*, August 2, 2024, charlesmastroni.com/ transinolympics.

biological females. The result is that these transgender athletes broke all kinds of records in swimming and other sports.[56]

Authorities believe in the so-called scientific truth of transgenderism. If you disagree with their idol, you are vilified and attacked as transphobic. In the arena of athletics, this is entirely unjust to biological women who have diligently trained for years to compete fairly in women's sports. All things being equal, when males and females are both in their prime, the best women cannot match the best men in any sport where physical strength, speed and power are an advantage. Without a doubt, a large, strong woman could defeat a much smaller man in a contest where physical strength is a key factor. However, this is not a fair comparison. Weight class also matters in sports like boxing, wrestling and mixed-martial arts.

Age influences performance too, since athletic ability diminishes over time. There is no question that a woman in her prime can outcompete a significantly older male. For example, in 1973, Billie Jean King, a top-ranked women's tennis player at age twenty-nine, defeated Bobby Riggs, a former champion, age fifty-five, who was far past his prime.[57] However, this wasn't a fair competition in any sense of the word. A young person in their prime will invariably beat someone who is older, regardless of their gender. Billie Jean King should have faced the top-ranked men's tennis player and winner of the US Open in 1971, who was Stan Smith.[58]

Men typically have a physical advantage over women in track and field and many other sports. Yet the progressive idol seeks to deny this reality, prioritizing the social engineering "truth" (another idol) that a biological male who identifies as a woman should compete against actual women—often dominating them.

---

[56] Christie Aschwanden, "Trans Athletes Are Posting Victories and Shaking Up Sports," *WIRED*, October 29, 2019, charlesmastroni.com/transathletevictories.
[57] Jesse Greenspan, "'Battle of the Sexes': When Billie Beat Bobby," *History*, updated May 28, 2025, charlesmastroni.com/billiejeanking.
[58] Richard Finn, "50 for 50: Stan Smith, 1971 Men's Singles Champion," *US Open*, March 6, 2018, charlesmastroni.com/stansmith.

To be clear, in the Bible and in Christian morality, women and men are equal. Both are made in the image of God, and they are purposefully different in many ways. And with the French, I say, "Vive la différence." Our basic instincts, our experiences, and our own two eyes see and know this. Yet the highly educated experts have a different truth they want to force on everyone. The equality of the sexes movement morphed into the fluidity of gender and an insistence that there is absolutely no difference between men and women, and an individual can switch back and forth based on their feelings. The authorities and experts are redefining the words *he, she* and *they* to meet the perceived needs of a few individuals.

Again, this idol is being propagated in our schools to young children and causing confusion, simply because authorities insist on rejecting the basic truth that there are males and females, boys and girls, men and women. These are the highly educated experts, the high priests of progressive knowledge and truth. They must know more than nature itself because we have now evolved, supposedly.

> And since they did not see fit to acknowledge God, God gave them up to a debased mind to do what ought not to be done. They were filled with all manner of unrighteousness, evil, covetousness, malice. They are full of envy, murder, strife, deceit, maliciousness. They are gossips, slanderers, haters of God, insolent, haughty, boastful, inventors of evil, disobedient to parents, foolish, faithless, heartless, ruthless (Romans 1:28–31).

Many of these same qualities apply to the progressive woke community, which denies God's reality and seeks to replace it with its own, attempting to play God with the human race.

Look at what radical environmentalists have done to promote their cause. Somehow, they have become convinced by their idol (science) that another of their idols (the Earth) is doomed if we don't reverse climate change by 2031, as a prominent federal representative predicted in 2019.[59] To get the world's attention, supporters defaced classic art.[60] This irrational behavior is based on a false belief promoted by the high priests (scientists) of the idol of environmentalism, acting as if they fully understand the planet's ecosystem.

Before the global warming scare, scientists were vigorously claiming an impending ice age by the twenty-first century.[61] Media picked up this cry with fear-mongering articles in *The New York Times*,[62] *The Washington Post*,[63] and *Time*.[64] Even though they did not have it all figured out, they claimed disaster was around the corner if you did not obey them. And when one of their warnings failed to come to pass, they rarely revisited the topic.

Other scientists predicted that if we did not control the many causes of acid rain on a global scale, all the trees and much of the wildlife would die.[65] But this did not happen. Academia highly touted these theories, while news outlets, television, movies and self-proclaimed conscientious celebrities amplified them through extensive media attention. Thus, the beliefs of this scientific idol

---

[59] John Bowden, "Ocasio-Cortez: 'World will end in 12 years' if climate change not addressed," *The Hill*, January 22, 2019, charlesmastroni.com/climatecatastrophe.

[60] Vittoria Benzine, "Here Is Every Artwork Attacked by Climate Activists This Year, From the 'Mona Lisa' to 'Girl With a Pearl Earring'," *Artnet News*, October 31, 2022, charlesmastroni.com/activistvandalism.

[61] Myron Ebell and Steven J. Milloy, "Wrong Again: 50 Years of Failed Eco-pocalyptic Predictions," Competitive Enterprise Institute, September 18, 2019, charlesmastroni.com/21stciceage.

[62] Robert Reinhold, "Foe of Pollution Sees Lack of Time; Asserts Environmental Ills Outrun Public Concern," *The New York Times*, August 10, 1969, charlesmastroni.com/pollution.

[63] Victor Cohn, "U. S. Scientist Sees New Ice Age Coming," *Washington Post*, July 9, 1971, charlesmastroni.com/iceageprediction.

[64] *Time*, "Another Ice Age?," June 24, 1974, charlesmastroni.com/anothericeage.

[65] Jack Reed, "Decade-Long Study: Acid Rain Not a Crisis," *Tampa Bay Times*, updated October 17, 2005, charlesmastroni.com/acidrain.

became a noble cause. This is how a partial truth presents itself as objective and gains power from proclaiming itself as absolute truth.

I can almost hear the serpent in the garden whispering, "You can be equal to God, knowing what is good and bad for everybody. You are wise enough. Go ahead and play God. Take control of everyone and tell them what they must do to survive." The false religion of environmentalism has followed the same pattern: scare people with the threat of death, suffering and the end of the world. Take advantage of the general cultural trust and belief in science and technology to gain power, influence, money or control. In other words, play God, or at least the role of a high priest of a powerful idol. The climate zealots have made catastrophic predictions that have scared the younger generation in the same way that the threat of nuclear war scared mine.

According to science, life on Earth began with a single-celled organism roughly 4.3 billion (or 4,300,000,000) years ago.[66] Yet global temperatures have only been systematically measured since about AD 1850.[67] That means scientists have less than two hundred years of standardized climate data. This is a minuscule sample, representing only 0.0000000047 of the time life has existed on Earth. Throughout that vast span, our planet has endured countless geological upheavals, such as multiple ice ages, meteor strikes, volcanic eruptions, and cycles of warming and cooling, yet it has continued to sustain life for all these years.

There are still approximately two million known species on Earth today, including robust populations of mammals, birds, reptiles, amphibians and fish.[68] Even when certain large species, such as the buffalo in North America, were nearly wiped out,

---

[66] Steve Koppes, "The Origin of Life on Earth, Explained," *University of Chicago News*, last reviewed November 2025, charlesmastroni.com/earthage.
[67] "A short history of measuring temperature," *MathBench: Climate Change–Hockey Stick*, University of Maryland, accessed January 9, 2026, charlesmastroni.com/measuringtemps.
[68] Hannah Ritchie, "How Many Species Are There?," *Our World in Data*, November 30, 2022, charlesmastroni.com/speciescount.

others endured. This demonstrates the remarkable resilience of Earth's ecosystems to sustain life despite both natural and man-made disruptions. As a Christian, I view this as evidence of God's design: just as he created the human body with the capacity to heal, he designed the Earth with the resilience to support and renew life.

I am convinced that a Chicken Little University somewhere is teaching scientists that the sky is falling somehow and soon. They take measurements with their models that they think are key to the whole system, extrapolate them into absolute truth, and predict disastrous outcomes. Do scientists really believe they understand the entire ecosystem of the Earth, past and present? Many seem to think they know how everything works and that their computer models are perfect predictors of coming disasters. And so, they sound the alarm. But is it true? Scientists may do this with good intentions, but they are only human, not God. They did not create the universe, and they do not know everything. The Christian belief is that the world will end when God chooses to end it, and not a second before. This is not in man's control but in God's.

Equally problematic is the field of genetics. Now that the human genome is mapped, researchers are evaluating what all the genes do and modifying them for medical treatments. Scientists, believing they are improving humankind, feel free to manipulate it all. Yet they don't know everything. Their computer models are built on incomplete knowledge and inevitably reflect their biases.

Likewise, since the interactions among genes are not fully understood, altering even one, no matter the reason, may carry unknown consequences, including potentially serious and harmful side effects. And if psychologists believe behavior can be genetically modified, that is truly scary.[69]

I am not suggesting we ignore scientific knowledge. We are given intelligence and are supposed to make discoveries and use them for good. But some humility is in order, and we need to

---

[69] Muhammad Tuhin, "How Genes Influence Your Behavior," *Science News Today,* April 21, 2025, charlesmastroni.com/geneinteractions.

understand that our knowledge is incomplete. As such, we should proceed with some caution, wisdom and respect for our Creator, who does know all. We must stop trying to take over everyone's lives through governmental power.

Yes, science and technology are probably the most influential idols in these times. Look at the hopes and fears surrounding AI. Proponents always focus on the potential benefits that can come from technology. However, our track record for anticipating unintended consequences is terrible and speaks for itself. The truth is that powerful and influential people are anticipating AI can solve most, if not all, of our problems. They are more than willing to subject us to their assumptions. If this is not a man-made god, I don't know what is.

Progressive people like to depict those who are religious as sheep, blindly following a creed. Well, I have news for every single one of us. Each person is a sheep, following what they believe in. This is inevitable—as sure as $2 + 2 = 4$. Our beliefs run our lives because they control our thoughts, feelings and actions. Beliefs and worldviews shape our choices and influence what we accept or reject as truth. That's why we must take time to examine them and be willing to question whether they actually reflect reality. I prefer to follow God's wisdom, which has stood the test of time and remains relevant today.

Is idolatry confined to ancient, ignorant people? Hardly. The individuals of those times built their graven man-made images around creation stories and moral codes. They accepted a central truth and used it to shape their civilizations, establish laws, and guide their lives and minds. Progressive, post-Christian thought does much the same. It carries identical elements, but its foundation rests on the belief that either God does not exist or that he is not needed to explain our existence and that the human mind is the only mind that counts.

The overarching banner of progressivism includes global warming, banning fossil fuels, and the benefits of diversity, equity and inclusion for all imagined genders. In the same way, the religion of progressivism requires that everyone should comply with its gods, its version of the truth, whether they are followers or not. Progressive beliefs, right or wrong, drive people to control other individuals and societies. And just like the idols of ancient times, their beliefs often led to human sacrifice—even the sacrifice of children.

We tend to think we have evolved past such abominations in the twenty-first century. However, look at what the gender mutilation of children has done under the name of gender-affirming care and the idols of science and psychology. One study tracked more than 48,000 patients in the US who had gender-affirming operations in hospitals and same-day surgery centers from 2016 through 2020. The number of surgical patients nearly tripled from 4,552 in 2016 to 13,011 in 2019. Amid the coronavirus restrictions of 2020, that number decreased slightly since many types of nonemergency operations were postponed or halted. Gender-affirming surgeries were most common among young adults; more than 25,000 people, ages nineteen to thirty, received these procedures. Just under 8 percent of patients (a total of 3,678) were twelve- to eighteen-year-olds.[70]

Also, consider what the idol of the pro-choice movement has done. Millions of children's lives have been sacrificed, over half a million every year in the US alone.[71] Are all these because of physical danger to the mother's health, or are most of them simply contraception? Conception uninterrupted becomes a baby. That is objective truth. Since the human race has survived and flourished, it follows that most pregnancies do not threaten the life of the

---

[70] Ken Alltucker, "More people are getting gender-affirming care, under attack in many states. Few are kids," *USA Today*, updated August 23, 2023, charlesmastroni.com/transkidstats.

[71] Jeff Diamant, Besheer Mohamed, and Rebecca Leppert, "What the Data Says About Abortion in the US," *Pew Research Center*, March 25, 2024, charlesmastroni.com/usabortion.

mother. On the other hand, I know many women who have fallen for pro-choice doctrine and have regretted it later.

Look at the nature-worshipping environmental movement. The zealots are absolutely willing to sacrifice jobs, food sources, and anything else they deem harmful to the environment—their god of climate change. They are doing their best to pass laws and regulations to enforce their beliefs on you, me and the whole world. They are fervent evangelists of a false god.

This brings us to so many social justice causes that have become idols of post-Christian Western cultures. Many of these causes started out as good and noble to make legitimate and necessary changes to our societies. However, they often turn into idols when taken to the extreme. Proponents of many social ideologies have some insight, but lack a full understanding of good and evil, and they underestimate the unethical side of human nature. Yet if they believe they know everything, this will typically result in an idol.

The civil rights movement was both necessary and right. It brought vital changes to our society and culture. For too long, African Americans had been discriminated against, persecuted and even killed in the US. The movement gained strength through the churches of the 1950s and 1960s, even amid intense opposition and suffering. Its most prominent leader, the Reverend Dr. Martin Luther King Jr., preached from a deeply Christian conviction that all people are equal in the eyes of God. He famously declared that we should not be judged by the color of our skin, but by the content of our character, envisioning a day when we could all sit together in brotherhood.[72] Dr. King championed nonviolent resistance as the means to achieve lasting change. These were righteous and necessary struggles. Yet, as often happens with the best of causes, time has led some to elevate the movement itself into an idol.

As I write this in 2025, those claiming to promote civil rights are practicing racism against their perceived oppressors, becoming

---

[72] History.com editors, "'I Have a Dream' Speech," *History*, updated March 5, 2025, charlesmastroni.com/mlkdream.

the very thing they claim to fight against. They went from King's speech of "I have a dream that all God's children can sit down at the table of brotherhood..." to CRT, which claims that the White race is inherently evil and racist. Judging and condemning others by the color of their skin is racism, regardless of color. The theory uses the terms *Whiteness* and *White privilege*, declaring Caucasians need to apologize for being White and acknowledge their Whiteness. CRT has become what King fought against. He argued for real justice based on Christian truth. However, CRT seeks retribution and aims to oppress its perceived oppressor. However, this does not result in justice or peace. It only results in continued strife and animosity. Where God's justice drove King, revenge and political power drive CRT.

Another example of a worthy cause that has been turned into idolatry is the women's rights movement, which was essential in securing equal pay, opportunity and respect for women, acknowledging them as equals capable of responsible and effective leadership. It rightly opposed the treatment of women as sexual objects and condemned sexual harassment in the workplace or anywhere else. Of course, women should not be treated as sexual objects. However, over time, some advocates pushed these ideals to an extreme, elevating women's rights above those of others. For example, an article in *Psychology Today* offered a feminist critique of marriage, portraying family life as being harmful to women and advocating that women owe it to themselves to break free of these chains.[73] In this view, the goal shifted from equality to superiority. Men and maleness were cast as the enemy, the historical oppressors of women. The promoters of this ideology criticized all traditional female roles, even those that had been desirable and called a blessing for most of human history.

Continuing this philosophy, childbearing and motherhood limited a woman's potential and earning power. Therefore, it must

---

[73] Neel Burton, MD, "A Feminist Critique of Marriage," *Psychology Today,* updated June 24, 2024, charlesmastroni.com/feministcritique.

be possible to address an unwanted pregnancy with the right to abort a child for the well-being of a woman, even up to full term and regardless of whether the child is viable if taken by C-section, solely based on a woman's right to choose. However, women did not create life, and they don't own the life growing in them. God created life, and every life has a father too. This demonstrates how a movement that initially started well was taken to the extreme, idolizing women and denigrating men while sacrificing children.

The loudest voices of the feminist movement hold that men have caused most of the problems in the world throughout history. Pejorative terms include maleness, paternalistic, male aggression, testosterone-fueled, and misogynistic. The original movement turned from equality between the sexes to the superiority of women over men. The belief that one gender is superior or inferior is sexist. Wasn't this the original issue? This is much the same pattern as CRT blaming all the problems in the world on Whiteness. Feminism just substitutes maleness.

These legitimate causes legally started out as civil rights issues and morally as human rights issues based on race and gender, but then they were extrapolated into idols. Other groups copied the pattern, claiming their ideologies were civil rights. This became the backbone of the morality of the progressive movement. And they pushed their idols into law wherever possible. Their morality is steeped in the lie told at the fall of humanity: that we can be equal with God, understanding good and evil without him. What started with just causes never stopped as it progressed to denigrating its perceived enemies and becoming the very thing they originally detested, becoming racist and sexist themselves.

Those who believe in God hold that he is the ultimate source of truth, reality and morality. According to God's design, marriage, love and procreation are united as one. From the beginning of humanity, this has been his intent, and for most of history, societies have lived in alignment with it. These three elements—marriage, love and the creation of new life—were never meant to be separated. Babies are to be conceived, born and raised within the marriage of a man and woman, providing them with stability and gendered role models. God's design establishes a small but vital community of trust, learning and love, where children can grow to appreciate and respect both men and women. A healthy traditional family equips its progeny to become responsible, compassionate adults and contributing members of society.

We are called to teach our children about God and to remind them they are a precious gift of life entrusted to our care. The ideal model is the sacrament of marriage, which has been honored across cultures since the beginning of the human race. Even modern psychology affirms the benefits of children growing up in traditional two-parent families compared to those raised in divorced and single-parent households. One study found the following.

> The studies conducted two to three decades back showed that family instability can negatively affect children's development. The absence or loss of one parent and conflicts between separated and divorced parents affect not only the child's mental health but also the child's physical health, overall growth, and future relationships. Single parents are often overburdened with the responsibilities of two parents, face social stigma, and lack social support, as a result they have difficulty spending time with their children. Hence, children of single parents have poor academic performance, decreased social interactions, emotional and behavioral problems.[74]

---

[74] Kersi Chavda and Vinyas Nisarga, "Single Parenting: Impact on Child's Development," *Journal of Indian Association for Development of Child and Adolescent Mental Health* 19, no. 1 (2023):14–20, doi.org/10.1177/09731342231179017.

Remember, in Genesis 1:28, God instructed us to "be fruitful and multiply," and later in Genesis 2:24, he clearly states a man and his wife are to become one flesh. According to the Creator's design, the power, pleasure and intimacy of sex are meant to be enjoyed. He does not make mistakes, and he made no mistake when he completed his creation.

In God's design for truth, reality and morality, any use of sex outside his intention, including before marriage, is wrong. We are not entitled to it, and we won't die if we don't have it. Though it is one of humanity's strongest desires, sex itself has become an idol in our culture, worshipped and distorted from its original purpose. According to God's commandments, adultery violates his moral law. He designed marriage to unite a man and a woman as one, bonding together in spiritual, emotional and physical union, so they might bring forth new life and raise their children according to God's will. Incidentally, in some states, the law recognizes couples who cohabitate long enough to be called "common-law married," declaring them husband and wife.

By God's design, marriage cannot be between two men or two women because these unions cannot produce life. Sex outside of marriage, adultery, and homosexual sex are contrary to his will for us. This includes couples who cohabitate without being married, many of whom have children together. Instead of a husband and wife raising children in a committed home, we have a lot of "baby daddy" and "baby mommy" situations, with unmarried parents living together and others apart. How can such noncommittal arrangements serve the best interests of children?

God is wiser than we are, including academics and the progressive movement. He knows what is best for his created people. That is why marriage has been God's will for humankind since the beginning. For virtually every culture in history, from tribal communities to developed societies, this truth and moral order went unquestioned until progressives vigorously promoted their own concepts of truth and morality.

I fully understand that questioning sexuality is not a popular idea to progressive thinkers, but until 2004, same-sex marriage wasn't officially recognized in the United States.[75] In 2001, the Netherlands was the first country to recognize it officially.[76] For thousands of years before that, marriage was solely between a man and a woman. But progressives insist that is wrong and the law should be otherwise.

What happened to make that change? One reason is that human ingenuity, beginning with the invention of condoms, enabled the conception of new life to be separated from the pleasure of sex, and ultimately marriage. We enjoy our sexual pleasure a lot, and this development was attractive because it removed the natural outcome of sex: the conception of children. Society could then enjoy their pleasure without any lasting consequences, like unwanted pregnancies, especially outside of marriage. Medical technology has added to the means of contraception with the development of birth control pills, vasectomies, tubal ligations, and the day-after pill.

This marked an early stop on the train of new beliefs. In addition, popular culture—romantic books, movies and television shows—promotes the idea that emotional love dominates our motivation in relationships. This message is especially prevalent in Western culture, where love is portrayed as being irresistible and deserving of fulfillment, regardless of plot twists, adultery, circumstances or consequences. Over time, many of these artistic cultural influences began championing the cause of homosexuality, using media to shape how audiences should think and feel about it.

The next stop on this belief train is the idea that sex is simply about pleasure—"sex is just sex," whether with the same or opposite sex. The message became, "It's all love, isn't it?" In this

---

[75] History.com editors, "Gay Marriage," *History*, updated May 28, 2025, charlesmastroni.com/gaymarriage.

[76] Hannah Ritchie, "More than 30 countries have legalized same-sex marriage," Our World in Data, May 17, 2024, charlesmastroni.com/netherlands.

view, God's design for men and women grew increasingly detached from marriage. To the progressive mindset, God was in the way, and religion was biased and prejudicial. As a result, popular culture came to portray sex as being purely physical, to be enjoyed with anyone a person is attracted to, disconnected from love, commitment or purpose. Casual hookups became normalized, with apps dedicated to facilitating them.

Once homosexuality was established as a civil right, it became the final stop on this belief train. Gay marriage is now legally sanctioned in many Western countries, promoted under the banner of the religion of progressivism. The latest tenet of this religion is accepting all of its idols. Using the same civil rights framework, the causes of all the LGBTQIA+ groups are being pressed into becoming law.

The pantheon of progressive idols has different ideas of what is true, right and moral for everyone. On the heels of the civil rights movements for race and women's equality, the progressive movement quickly claimed its own moral truths and has pushed those onto the rest of us. Progressives with a religious background will even selectively interpret Scripture to suit their beliefs, not God's well-established truth.

These woke beliefs stand in clear contrast to believing in a creator. If you know God created you, you are grateful for the body he gave you and accept he has a claim on you. We may not have the greatest bodies, but we are alive. Nor do we will ourselves into existence. We don't even will our hearts to pump—they just do. However, we do the best we can with the bodies we have.

Yet, if someone doesn't believe in God, then they don't believe they owe anyone for their life (except maybe their biological parents). That belief train leads to the conclusion that one can be whatever one wants to be, regardless of whether God made them.

The woke truths of gender dysphoria—transgender, gender fluidity, and nonbinary identities—claim our gender is not determined by our bodies, despite overwhelming evidence to the contrary. LGBTQIA+ individuals deserve protection from persecution. However, that doesn't mean these beliefs benefit the individual or society. Promoting and celebrating these identities cannot be considered progress for humankind. By Darwinian standards, it is not even evolution, since these groups are less likely to bear offspring, which is the core principle of Darwin's theory.

Returning to God's design, marriage, sex and procreation are all part of the same concept. Heterosexual intercourse is the physical connection to the miracle of life and unites the spirits of a man and a woman. The spirit gives life to the body, not the other way around. God created and designed both of them. As a result, we are spiritually and physically connected with our children from the moment of conception. God's plan is to fill the earth with people. On this practical level, what is best for the human race? Marriage, sex and procreation have been debated under the banner of the already accepted civil rights movements rather than being considered as basic and fundamental natural truths. Progressivism is not progress. The progressive woke insist the world must conform to their viewpoint and anthropological ideas, despite the evidence of nature itself.

Here is a summary of many clear, objective truths:

1. Heterosexual relationships can naturally produce life, usually without medical intervention, while same-sex relationships cannot.

2. People and higher animals are born male or female to continue their respective species and do not naturally change genders.

3. Until recently, marriage was unquestionably between a man and a woman.

4. There must be objective truth and reality, or there is no truth or reality.

5. Internal feelings or beliefs can be true and real or false and illusions. However, personal beliefs about truth do not change objective truth. We can believe either what is true or what is false.

For stating the simple truth, many will hate me and call me evil. This is because those who believe falsehoods hate the truth and fight for their version of it, their idol god. Belief runs deep in each one of us, right down to our core. Therefore, people feel personally attacked if their views are challenged. But maintaining lies and falsehoods is harmful, especially when forcing them onto others.

So who is really more judgmental? If you disagree with the progressive woke movement and cancel culture, you are often branded as any combination of derogatory terms, including transphobic, homophobic, misogynistic, bigoted, a religious nut, backward, unenlightened, unevolved, a troglodyte, ignorant or uninformed. Even though the five facts stated above are observable and have been true throughout the thousands of years of human existence, the self-appointed progressives insist on imposing a new truth for society, and they attack, vilify and try to ruin anyone who stands in their way. Their judgmentalism and resulting anger empowers a false sense of moral superiority in them. This makes people feel strong, and their self-righteous posture treats dissent as something to be silenced rather than discussed or debated.

How can I get along and be accepted by the progressive woke? As a White Christian male, I would stand a better chance if I identified as something else. If I were to identify as a "furry," someone who adopts animal persona, then they would have to accept me. Since the elephant is an endangered species, maybe I should identify as one. After all, in writing this book, I'm pointing out the elephant in the room (and I'm somewhat overweight). Or what about another endangered species, the polar bear? I am certainly poking the bear with my words.

On a more serious note about identification, let's consider Rachel Dolezal.[77] Rachel was born a White girl to White parents and raised in Montana. At an early age, she became fascinated with African American culture and the racial injustice toward Black Americans. She identified so closely with this noble cause that she claimed to be a Black woman. Yet when her parents were interviewed, they told the world she was Caucasian and of German, Czech and Swedish descent.

Admirably, she wanted to fight for civil rights. She became chapter president for the National Association for the Advancement of Colored People (NAACP) in Spokane, Washington, and a university instructor in Africana Studies. She changed her appearance to look more like a Black woman with darker skin and hair, even though she was naturally a blonde-haired, blue-eyed White girl. In interviews, she even claimed repeatedly—to authorities, students, universities, the NAACP—that an African American man was her biological father. Later, her true ancestry became known.

She sympathized and empathized with African Americans on a deep personal level. There is nothing wrong with that. In fact, it is noble and admirable. But that does not make her a Black woman, no matter how much she wants to be one. Strong feelings or desires do not change reality.

A person can want something so intensely that they may convince themselves and others of something that is, in fact, not true. Many White civil rights activists have passionately believed in the cause of justice for African Americans. You do not have to be Black to seek fairness and justice for others or to work tirelessly for that cause. However, when a Caucasian girl yearns so deeply to be a Black woman that she pretends to be one, it becomes a delusion. It simply isn't the case.

---

[77] ABC News, "Rachel Dolezal: A Timeline of the Ex-NAACP Leader's Transition From White to 'Black'," *ABC News*, June 16, 2015, charlesmastroni.com/dolezal.

To get along with the progressives, should I identify as a Black male victim of White society even though I'm White? You might say that's impossible. But what if I assert that this is how I identify and that it reflects who I am inside? Who are you to question my chosen reality? Isn't that situation similar to transgenderism? Someone believes, or becomes convinced by social media or authority figures, that they are the opposite gender from their biological sex. They may sincerely believe it, but why must everyone else accept it? Why is it labeled as "hate speech" if I refuse to endorse their reality and pronouns?

If someone wants or believes themselves to be a different gender, they may adopt this identity based on their internal sense of self. Like Rachel Dolezal, a person might want something so strongly that they believe it to be so, but that does not alter objective reality. We are not solely psychological beings; we exist in physical bodies as well. The underlying and unspoken claim is that rather than being created by God, you can create yourself. But is this really true?

Strong feelings can be dead wrong. Our beliefs are built on basic, fundamental realities, and to think otherwise is more delusion than reality. It is only through the influence of the hyperintelligent academics and PhDs that this fundamental truth has been questioned.

These lies and untruths are cloaked in deceptive language (terms like gender-affirming care, concern, love, inclusiveness, kindness, protecting the vulnerable, civil rights, and equity). All are noble-sounding platitudes and towers to heaven. While many began as worthy causes, whatever good intentions they may have had when these belief trains started down the tracks, they have since veered off course from reality. Our beliefs shape our lives, guiding us in every action we take. Therefore, it is crucial that both individuals and societies are grounded in real, true and wise beliefs.

> Then God said, "Let us make mankind in our image,
> in our likeness, so that they may rule over the fish

in the sea and the birds in the sky, over the livestock
and all the wild animals, and over all the creatures
that move along the ground" (Genesis 1:26 NIV).

The promoters of progressivism aim to remake humankind in their own image, based on their beliefs, their self-proclaimed truths. They are willing to wield political power to impose their worldview on you. Ultimately, you must believe something. So, what do you believe, and is it true?

Idols are everywhere, gods of our invention,
New truths to capture our attention.

Our belief and acceptance they demand.
They promise progress is at hand.

Their cause is urgent and most pressing.
Don't question, no second-guessing.

They are crying, "the planet is dying."
If you deny it, you are lying.

Everything is social injustice.
You're a racist homophobe if you don't trust us.

Don't agree with your genitalia?
Our scalpels and hormones won't fail ya.

If self-fulfillment is your aim,
Come to us and we will train.

You don't need God; we will do.
Art and science can now guide you.

Idols want your heart, mind, soul and body.
But trusting them is pure folly.

The Nature of Lies and Truth

When we accept lies, we embrace a false reality, whether we are aware of it or not. This is not a healthy state of being. We may convince ourselves we don't need God and can craft our own reality, just like Adam and Eve in the garden. But is it truth? Do we genuinely understand and believe what is true? When we think we are fine and able without God, it amounts to a fundamental rejection of him, whether we intend to or not.

If the progressives can convince or pressure people into accepting their woke views, they feel validated, powerful, supported and right. They believe in their vision and desperately want it to be recognized as true and real. Consequently, they insist others accept their so-called truth. Many of these modern idols are trying to alter the Creator's reality and morality.

The more they can persuade or intimidate others into agreeing with them, the more powerful, validated and justified they feel. Yet only God determines what is actually true. We can either accept what is real as he has made it, or choose to live in deception. Falsehood is simply an attempt to replace truth with illusion. For example, when someone steals and then claims "It was always mine" or "It should be mine," they are trying to convince both others and themselves that the stolen item rightfully belongs to them. But despite their wishes, it is not truly theirs. They want it enough to steal it, and if they aren't caught or seen, they craft their own new reality: the item is now theirs.

But God sees them because he is omniscient. He knows the item in question is not really theirs—they have stolen it. From our limited human perspective, however, if a lie isn't exposed to the light, it can easily masquerade as truth. Meanwhile, the actual owner suffers from the loss of the item and the erosion of trust with fellow humans, which signifies deeper spiritual damage. Unless someone with authority (for example, a parent or a judge) believes the truth (that the item belongs to the real owner), the victim might not see justice. We are taught, "You shall not steal" (Exodus 20:15). This is the eighth commandment of God, a reminder that he knows what we do. There can be no justice without objective truth, and at the end of our days, God ensures justice is served.

Other examples of falsehoods always involve attempts to create one's reality, which isn't possible. When someone murders another, they may try to cover it up by lying, tampering with evidence, concocting a story to prove their innocence, providing a false alibi, or fleeing the scene. The murderer tries to throw the authorities off track, hoping they will believe a different reality than the one that truly unfolded. Yet, we are told, "You shall not murder" (Exodus 20:13). This is the sixth commandment of God, another reminder that he knows what we do. Again, there can be no justice without objective truth. In the end, God ensures justice prevails because he knows what is real.

If authorities discover what actually happened, the perpetrator will be arrested and brought to trial. The evidence will prove the murderer's guilt to a judge and jury, allowing the family and friends to receive some measure of justice here and now. The murderer may be punished, but of course, the victim is not restored to life.

Some people fabricate stories about their accomplishments to appear more impressive than they are. They brag because they want you to believe them so they can win your admiration. Others invent tragic hardships to gain sympathy. They tell stories of how difficult their life has been and lie so you believe they are heroic for persevering under made-up duress. This is reverse bragging. In both cases, they are manipulating perception, attempting to construct an alternate reality for others to believe.

In creating a false narrative, they are building on lies that inevitably collapse. When they ignore the truth long enough, holding on to their false beliefs, they become truly delusional, living in a fantasy they fiercely defend. When confronted, they often become offended or angry and attack anyone who questions their narrative. Or they seek new audiences willing, at least temporarily, to believe their illusion. This is a pattern we see among progressives, as well as politicians.

My goodness, if there were ever a group that intentionally tries to convince you to believe their supposed truth, it is politicians. "When I am elected, I will ————." Do they ever speak honestly? More often than not, they say whatever they think will earn your trust so you'll grant them power.

CHAPTER 8

The Idols of Progressivism

On a lesser scale, we all lie about our lives to some extent. We embellish past escapades and downplay our faults, all to make ourselves appear better than we are. We present a good face in front of others, putting our best foot forward or just hiding our faults, but this has far less impact on society than what progressive activists and social engineers are attempting.

Several modern man-made gods were mentioned earlier in this book. Yet in the first commandment, God says: "I am the Lord your God … You shall have no other gods before me." (Exodus 20:2–3). How do lies and an alternate belief system play out in these progressive causes? God created reality. When a partial truth is accepted as the whole truth, it is still a lie, and when intelligent people plausibly present one, it becomes the worst kind of lie because it is believable. These falsehoods can easily masquerade as objective reality. They deceive many because such lies have a seed of truth to them.

The cultural idol worshippers identify a piece of reality, like observable problems in society, and expand it to be the overriding truth of life. Everything is then viewed and interpreted through this lens. For example, today's social justice idol, which claims racism is ever-present, began with a real and serious truth: the historical injustice and prejudice that denied African Americans the same freedoms and pursuit of happiness enjoyed by other US citizens. Leaders like Rev. Dr. Martin Luther King Jr. preached and marched for equality, acceptance and equal opportunities for African Americans.[78] Laws were passed, such as the Civil Rights Act of 1964, that prohibited discrimination due to race, color, religion, sex or national origin. This act also established the Equal Employment Opportunity Commission to prevent employment discrimination. Additional laws and court rulings prohibited segregation in schools and outlawed hate crimes.

Rev. Dr. Martin Luther King Jr. was not the only pastor involved in the civil rights movement. Rev. Ralph Abernathy, Rev. Fred Shuttlesworth, Rev. Joseph Lowery and Rev. Howard Thurman were also prominent civil rights leaders as well. Their righteousness and strength came from their faith in God, who created all people. And they wanted the same freedom and equality that the Declaration of Independence promised for all Americans.

> We hold these truths to be self-evident, that all men are created equal, that they are endowed by their Creator with certain unalienable rights, that among these are Life, Liberty and the pursuit of Happiness.

The civil rights movement was rooted in Christianity and belief in God's truth. Malcolm X (a minister for the Nation of Islam) also preached that all people were equal and created by God. The efforts of these men and their followers touched the conscience of the nation and transformed the minds and hearts of the people to do what is right. American culture changed. Speeches were given, movies were filmed, and songs were written taking up this righteous cause.

But the present-day civil rights movement derives its authority from academia rather than God and rejects the idea that any change

---

[78] In my opinion, Martin Luther King was a prophet in the biblical sense, with a vision from God for the nation based on Christian truth.

has been made in people or the culture regarding racism and prejudice. Proponents claim there is systemic racism everywhere and in everything. They assert this even though we have many African American business leaders, politicians, celebrities, and elected officials at both the city and state level, including former President Barak Obama, who held the highest office in the land. A large percentage of military and police forces across the nation is made up of African Americans. Yet present-day civil rights leaders and Black Lives Matter supporters still claim racism is just as prevalent now as before. Even former President Biden has repeatedly stated that racism—including White supremacy—remains a serious and ongoing threat in America today.

However, the idol of ever-present racism started with an actual reality of injustice and prejudice. Laws were passed making segregation, discrimination and hate crimes illegal and punishable. Celebrities and artists showed their support for equality, and culture changed for the better when Rev. Dr. Martin Luther King Jr.'s vision became more of a reality.

The Idol of Critical Race Theory

Born in academia, critical race theory was a drastic change from what Martin Luther King preached, which was that we should be judged based on the content of our character, not the color of our skin. However, CRT denies any significant progress in reducing racism while branding all White people as intrinsically racist, whether they are or not. Those who believe this theory claim that White people must recognize and apologize for their Whiteness.[79]

Yet stereotyping and denigrating an entire race because of their skin color is racism, no matter what the color is. With persuasive language, CRT supporters have convinced many in government

---

[79] Nikki Lisa Cole, PhD, "The Definition of Whiteness in American Society," *ThoughtCo*, May 15, 2025, charlesmastroni.com/whiteness.

and corporate America to adopt their beliefs, even while becoming racists themselves.

For proponents of CRT, proving ever-present racism becomes their overriding purpose. They convince academic professors (their priests) to espouse their idol's religion, and they write books (their scriptures) claiming the whole truth. You are a racist (a heretic) if you disagree. They run social justice organizations for profit, book speaking engagements (sermons), get appointed to governmental agencies, and raise funds from corporations and private citizens (passing the plate). This is the pattern.

The initially legitimate cause of racial equality rooted in religion now changed those roots to Marxism, and Karl Marx was an atheist. Christianity says racism is morally wrong and all people are equal. Equity says everyone needs to have access to equal economic resources. If that means the government must redistribute wealth, supporters say, "Let's do it," which is the same as saying, "Amen."

The Idol of Environmentalism

The environmental movement has now become an idol. It started with real and observable concerns, such as severe air pollution in major cities, during the 1970s and waste disposal crises, like Love Canal, one of the worst chemical waste disasters in US history. There is no doubt the movement received legitimate support for legitimate problems.

But now proponents claim the world is ending, and climate change is an omnipresent existential threat that must be addressed at all costs, regardless of the rights of nations, individuals or any facts that challenge their narrative. This becomes their overriding purpose. Academic professors (their priests) espouse their idol's religion and write books (their scriptures), proclaiming that methane, carbon dioxide, carbon emissions, and fossil fuels are the problem. They act as though they fully understand the entire ecosystem of their god, Mother Earth. If you disagree, you are a climate denier (a heretic).

Environmental activists secure speaking engagements (sermons), grant money, appointments to governmental agencies, and funds from corporations (passing the plate) for their organizations promoting their cause along with promises to become carbon neutral (holy). Every time you breathe, you are contributing carbon dioxide to the atmosphere, and you yourself are part of the problem, offending the god of climate change. You too must be controlled to ensure you don't use too much energy, eat too much meat, or drive too far, among other things. This is the pattern.

Environmentalists seek to control everything to save the planet. Then the activists push to get laws passed, and now we have the Environmental Protection Agency with the power to shut down whatever they see as a problem. They mandate electric cars to replace fossil-fuel vehicles while ignoring the strip-mining required to obtain battery materials and the environmental impact of disposing of their toxic batteries. And that's just the harmful effects we're aware of now. The full truth about the total life-cycle effects of electric vehicles is still unknown. Again, they act like they know the entire ecosystem of their god, Nature, and their word is absolute truth. However, air pollution in major cities is well under control compared to the 1970s since we now have unleaded gas, fuel-efficient cars, and emissions controls and standards.[80] Electric cars are their present mission to establish carbon neutrality.

Since the environmentalist idol must grow in influence, its supporters promoted recycling our trash, which was also a reasonable idea at first. But then the regulations became so stringent that it became too expensive to dispose of garbage. As a result, local dumps could not afford to operate any longer and closed. Waste disposal became a problem that still is not solved, because we are putting trash on barges and dumping it at sea in

---

[80] "The Clean Air Act: Successes and Challenges Since 1970," *Resources for the Future*, January 6, 2020, charlesmastroni.com/cleanairact.

order to make landfills comply with their enviro-religion and the enviro-commandments, which defeats the original purpose.

The vegetarian and animal rights denominations supported the environmentalist cause because they don't want us to eat meat. The farting animals we eat are offending the god of the climate change denomination of the eco-religion with their methane flatulence. And ultimately, based on Darwinian thinking that people are no better than animals, the animal rights advocates joined the vegetarians in order to substitute protein from plants and insects instead of the meat we enjoy.[81] Yes, they want us to eat bugs.

There is scientific data contradicting all the enviro-religious denominations, but that does not stop activists. They advocate renewable and sustainable everything. For a long time, they suggested growing crops to make alcohol as a substitute for gasoline until someone calculated that this was not possible without taking so much farmland that we would not be able to feed ourselves or the animals we eat.

The Idol of Sex

How has free love worked out in our society? This idol elevates sex as a god to be indulged, and the desire for it must be obeyed. The Stephen Stills song "Love the One You're With," released in 1970, epitomizes this. Many families were destroyed or never formed because of free love (in other words, the unfettered indulgence of lust).

Another maxim of the 1960s that demonstrated this mindset is "Whatever two consenting adults do with their bodies is no one else's business." Again, sex is an idol. Self-indulgence and adultery were promoted and tolerated because of this belief. But look at the consequences. Sexually transmitted diseases (STDs) increased as a result of free love and, in the decades that followed, many

---

[81] Pascal Kwesiga, "Could grasshoppers really replace beef?," *BBC Future*, July 20, 2022, charlesmastroni.com/insectmeat.

lives were lost to AIDS (acquired immune deficiency syndrome). Adultery broke many marriages up, causing innocent children to suffer the effects of divorce.

Another result of the sexual revolution was to view intercourse as a physical act devoid of its fuller spiritual context. Sex increasingly became only for pleasure and lust, overtaking the spiritual reality of marriage and a husband and wife joining as one, with the possibility of creating the miracle of new life. But we wanted the pleasure of intercourse without any of the consequences of procreation, which led to the widespread use of contraceptives. By reducing sex to merely a physical act, the emotions of true love and bonding are lost in exchange for indulging physical pleasure. The prevalence of pornography on the internet is evidence of that.

Lust overshadows genuine love. I learned this the hard way in my late twenties because I was a child of the '60s and '70s, when the sexual revolution was in full swing. I woke up one morning with yet another woman I had no emotional connection with. This kind of life had no meaning, no goodness, and no future. It consisted only of physical pleasure and the next score. I didn't know it at the time, but this realization was part of God calling me back to him.

Sex is directly connected to life, and our spirits are involved because it is our spirit that gives life to the body. This is objective truth, and I was only experiencing the partial truth of the pleasure of sex. Believing this lie left me spiritually empty, and I am sure my sexual partners felt the same. That is why God instituted marriage in virtually every culture. Sex is more powerful than we realize. It can build up our spirits in a deep love relationship or end in heartbreak. It is so much more than mere physical pleasure.

Casual sex is present everywhere in entertainment media. It is viewed as a rite of passage. The mantra of the '60s and '70s was "If it feels good, do it. Don't be so uptight and prudish." And that idea is still prevalent in Western culture.[82]

---

[82] David D. Nowell, PhD, "If It Feels Good Do It?" *Psychology Today,* February 6, 2011, charlesmastroni.com/feelsgood.

In our children's public education, religious morality was removed and the school systems just gave into the idea that "They're going to have sex anyway, so let's teach them how to do it safely" and "Just teach them how to use condoms and birth control, so they don't get pregnant." Clearly, this lesson was not effective, since so many children are born outside of marriage.

I was born in 1954 and lived through these times. After a while, the cultural norm progressed as follows:

1. People accepted God's standard that abstinence is best until marriage.

2. Then, they adopted the idea that it is no one's business what two consenting adults do.

3. And now, sex is viewed as a rite of passage into adulthood.

Thinking that people should not engage in sex outside of marriage has been ridiculed as impossible because of the cultural changes ushered in during the sexual revolution. This doesn't even take into consideration the emotional damage done to the spirits of those who became promiscuous.

In addition, the number of STDs has skyrocketed as a result of forsaking God's way. Since 1981, deaths from the human immunodeficiency virus (HIV) total over forty-four million worldwide[83] with more than sixteen million AIDS orphans.[84] An estimated ninety-one million people have been infected globally.[85] This is not God intentionally punishing anyone. These results

---

[83] UNAIDS, *Global HIV & AIDS statistics—Fact sheet*, updated July 10, 2025, charlesmastroni.com/aidsfacts.

[84] Paula Braitstein et al., "Association of Care Environment With HIV Incidence and Death Among Orphaned, Separated, and Street-Connected Children and Adolescents in Western Kenya," *JAMA Network Open* 4, no. 9 (September 2021): e2125365, doi.org/10.1001/jamanetworkopen.2021.25365 (PMC 8446813).

[85] World Health Organization, "HIV: The Global Health Observatory," accessed January 9, 2026, charlesmastroni.com/whoonhiv.

derive naturally from our willfulness when we desire what is not good for us. It is the cause-and-effect of our actions when we make unwise choices.

The comprehensive sex education that was introduced into American schools was supposed to prevent STDs and unwanted pregnancies in teens and young adults. Now, sex education has supposedly evolved to include transgender education.

Ignoring God's fundamental objective truth has consequences. The statistics of births out of wedlock are staggering. In 2021, 1.46 million unmarried women became mothers in the US. That year, 40 percent of all births were out of wedlock. Among Whites, 27.5 percent of births were to unwed mothers, with 70 percent among Blacks, and 68.5 percent among Native Americans.[86] The percentages of these births categorized by the age of the mother were:

99.7 percent: under 15 years old

98.2 percent: 15–17

89.9 percent: 18–19

68.1 percent: 20–24

41.0 percent: 25–29[87]

The courts are barraged with child support cases, and many young children are not in a stable home with two parents. This has placed a tremendous burden on the welfare system, which was far less necessary prior to the revolution of the '60s and '70s with its free love. When most of the culture believed in God, there were fewer out-of-wedlock pregnancies, and STDs were much rarer compared to today. What if we still followed God's truth?

---

[86] "National Vital Statistics Reports: Births: Final Data for 2021," Centers for Disease Control, Volume 72, No. 1, January 31, 2023, charlesmastroni.com/birthdata, 5.

[87] "Births: Final Data for 2021," CDC, 27.

Other results of the idol of sexual indulgence include child pornography and molestation. This is one of the unintended consequences of the internet. Predators lie to children online, pretending to be their age. They groom them and, over time, convince them to send nude photos or meet up with them in person. Children are raised with entertainment that shows casual sex as the norm. The message that's sent is that "Sex is good. Don't be a prude." Culture plus peer pressure will often lead them to provide the requested images. Television programs like *Dateline* show what happens when they catch offenders in the act. This wickedness is widespread. But critics of such sting operations question the morality of catching and exposing the pedophiles in this way.[88] For some, the rights of pedophiles are more important than protecting these vulnerable children.

Child molesters indulge their god of sexual gratification by lying to children and abusing their trust. The more violent ones may then scare the child into not telling the truth by threatening to harm their families. Others may threaten to send their nude pictures to their classmates if they tell. These predators hide both the sin and the crime to claim sexual gratification for themselves. Along the way, they destroy the innocence of children by exploiting and sometimes even raping them.

The Idol of Drugs

How has the belief—and idol—of the so-called mind-expanding drug culture worked out in our society? This false belief destroyed how many lives after being promoted in song after song and movie after movie? As I mentioned before, Berkley professor Timothy Leary actively promoted this lifestyle of psychedelic drug use. "Tune in, turn on, and drop out" was the mantra of the day,

---

[88] David Wenger, "Entrapment or Vigilantism? The Legal Boundaries of Online Predator Hunting in Pennsylvania," *Attorney Wenger Blog*, July 25, 2024, charlesmastroni.com/predatorhunting.

and the same spirit of rebellion and self-indulgence that began with psychedelic experimentation (LSD) has continued through successive drug waves—from the hippie era to later drug epidemics involving heroin (1970s), cocaine (1980s), ecstasy (1990s), and methamphetamine (2000s–present).

The fundamental belief is that the idol of drugs will provide temporary pleasure or relief from a harsh reality, but it ignores that the truth always wins. Running from it offers false hope and a short-term escape. The modern term for this is self-medicating. Doesn't that sound nice? But self-medicating doesn't heal because reality is waiting when one crashes after the high. Since truth is eternal, that's what lasts.

The publicized escapades of the drug-induced behavior of popular rock groups were idolized, held up as these heroes rebelled against the man and the establishment. They are the high priests of the drug culture. But does this pursuit lead us anywhere other than self-destruction?

The Idols of Communism and Socialism

Communism is an idol as well as a political and social movement. Many believe in it instead of the freedom of the individual, mistakenly contrasting it with capitalism. But the true opposite of communism is freedom. Communism and its first cousin, socialism, uphold total state control, turning the state into a god with absolute power over the citizens' lives, supposedly to bring about good for all. In both systems, the state can grant or take away individual rights. By contrast, the founders of the United States insisted our Creator gives our rights and freedoms. Therefore, they come from an authority superior to the government. However, modern progressive idols have severely curtailed these God-given rights in the US.

The communist system collects all money and controls all businesses, doling out favoritism as the party sees fit. They tell everyone it will be fair and equitable—that is the sales pitch. But their leaders control all the goods and services, while money is taken from the workers and their labor is directed and controlled. The party propaganda becomes a substitute for truth and reality, and it is forced on people whenever a group gains enough power. They punish those who hold opposing views and discourage free thought or free speech. The communists in power are "more equal than others," as George Orwell points out in his book *Animal Farm*.

John Lennon's song "Imagine" is the Communist Manifesto put to music, by his own admission.[89] Its ideals were held up as a goal for the world to believe in and aspire to. The vision painted by Lennon's anthem to progressivism and communism made them sound appealing. Peace would reign when we came together and believed in a world that had no heaven or hell or countries or religions. He asked for no possessions, greed or hunger, sharing all the world together.

But what is the track record of communism? Communist regimes have become among the most violent systems of oppression: totalitarian governments employing imprisonment, forced labor, suppression of thought, and outright mass killings to maintain control. The Soviet Union under Lenin and Stalin exemplified how far it could go.

China was no different under Mao Tse Tung and is still completely totalitarian under Xi Jinping. Protesters at Tiananmen Square were crushed by China's military. And then there was Pol Pot in Cambodia and Castro in Cuba. Europe has adopted what is called "democratic socialism," and many promote this in the US. However, socialism is communism light, where the individual still has no rights or freedoms the government can't suspend or remove as it sees fit. And the state has the control to do anything it deems necessary for the common good. Instead of guns, socialism just uses the power of bureaucracy to control, tax, regulate, fine

---

[89] Joe Taysom, "The misunderstood meaning of iconic John Lennon song 'Imagine'," *Far Out Magazine*, December 14, 2020, charlesmastroni.com/imagine.

and punish its citizens for what the government views as "wrong" beliefs and speech.

In the UK, among other Western nations, people have been arrested for text messages that were deemed politically incorrect or considered to be hate speech. We speak our thoughts, so this is an attack on any free speech that may contradict the official acceptable thinking. This is the Thought Police right out of George Orwell's *1984*.

Look at what many progressive governments did with the COVID vaccines. If you did not comply, you could get fired from your job, could not do business with the government, could not assemble for worship, and could have your business shut down. When anyone disagreed with the progressive woke, they demanded to have them fired and canceled. There was no personal freedom of choice here.

Socialism is still rooted in Marx and Engels's Communist Manifesto, and the basic premise is that God does not exist and religion is the opium of the people. But roses do not grow from the roots of stinkweed, and neither will a flourishing society grow from Marx and Engels's philosophies, even if you call it socialism instead of communism.

Communism is a clear picture of what scripture depicts in the story of the Tower of Babel. All man-made philosophies are idols and become false gods when believed as the whole truth. God made humanity free, whether for better or worse. That is the truth.

What about the communes of the '60s and '70s? This was communism on a supposedly manageable scale. Most of them failed because people would not be responsible citizens of the community. They couldn't agree on an equal division of work or goods. What a surprise!

How can anyone still be naive about human nature after taking even one good look at history—or at life itself? Lennon made his imagined utopia sound so wonderful. But if you believe it, you are dreaming of a false reality. Humanity has a dark side, as both history and personal experience clearly show. And if we're honest with ourselves, we're not perfect enough for communism—or any utopia—because there are no perfect people or leaders. We all have some selfishness and pride, and we argue even with those we love, let alone with people we don't.

And who governs in communism? Where do we find perfect leaders who, while holding absolute power, will make everything equal and fair without favoring themselves or their families? Such people do not exist. Lennon dreams of no heaven, where everyone is perfect, yet denies the very faith that promises heaven to those who believe in God. In "Imagine," he also ignores hell and the dark side of human nature. Ironically, the promoters of communism and similar ideologies have no doubt they are perfect enough to rule everyone (leaders like Vladimir Lenin, Joseph Stalin, Fidel Castro, Chairman Mao, and Pol Pot).

If there were perfect human beings, it would be nice, but that is a sentimental fool's dream. Lennon, Marx, Engels and progressives attempt to build a man-made tower to heaven without God, just like the Tower of Babel in Genesis.

The Idol of Cults

As we finish addressing idolatry, we see smaller-scale Towers of Babel today in the form of cults. Here, the leaders provide a kind of personal Tower of Babel in their self-actualization philosophies. Many promise that you can control all aspects of your life, even your environment, because you attract it by what is within you. These cults promise a path to self-perfection—heaven on a personal level. The leader is typically considered divine or at least superior to the followers and serves as their god even if he or she does not claim that directly.

In cults hiding behind a Christian ideology, the leader often claims to be Jesus or God or to have a direct line to the Creator that only they possess. Jim Jones and the Jonestown Massacre are probably the most publicized, and later David Koresh of the Waco

Branch Davidians also became well known. Despite Jesus's warning that false leaders would claim to be him (Matthew 24:23–26), many of these individuals still declare they are Christ himself or possess divine power.

This phenomenon is not limited to false-Christian cult leaders. The Nation of Islam in the US has the anointed messengers Elijah Muhammad, Wallace D. Fard, and Louis Farrakhan. Radical Islam has its Bin Ladens, and the doomsday cult Aum Shinrikyo, based on Buddhism, Hinduism and yoga, had Asahara Shoko, who convinced his followers to use sarin gas in the Japanese subways. All these men turned out to be corrupt, using their power and falsified ideologies to dominate others, sexually abuse or control people, or rip them off monetarily.

And then there are the self-actualization idols and false prophets of the New Age cults, such as pseudospiritual, personal-growth power cults, like Scientology with L. Ron Hubbard, NXIVM with Keith Reniere, Buddhafield through Yoga with Jaime Gomez, and James Arthur Ray, who led three people to their death in a sweat lodge under the promise of self-fulfillment and self-actualization.[90] These self-improvement ideologies purport to lead people to personal power or a better version of themselves, based solely on their knowledge and practices. However, this puts all the burden completely on oneself, without God. But how can someone know themself without knowing their Maker?

New Age cults are based on a leader, who is limited by their own human ideas, will and effort. They take our natural abilities and purport to release godlike superabilities to control ourselves and our world by our efforts of will and discipline alone. In short, they promote the lie told by the serpent (Satan) at the origin of humanity: that they can be equal to God. If only we follow the leader, we will fully actualize ourselves and have the power to be anything we want.

---

[90] ABC News, "James Ray Found Guilty of Negligent Homicide in Arizona Sweat Lodge Case," *ABC News*, June 22, 2011, charlesmastroni.com/jamesray.

CHAPTER 9

The Limits of Human Goodness

The godless worldview that shapes secular culture has its roots in our fallen nature, as Genesis teaches. We believe we are as wise as God, and we don't truly need him. Instead of looking beyond the human mind for knowledge, we rely on science and technology, and increasingly turn to AI and secular philosophies for guidance. For moral direction, we look to psychology, the social sciences, and shifting cultural trends. For salvation, we try to build a heaven on earth through various idols—political systems, such as democracy, communism and socialism, along with social justice causes meant to correct the wrongs in the world. When confronted with wickedness, disorders or flaws within ourselves, we turn to psychology, medicine, neuroscience and genetics. And when these efforts fail, which they invariably do, we rely on laws, police enforcement, and imprisonment to maintain a civilized life. All of this leads to the unavoidable question: if we have so many tools, systems and experts at our disposal, why is the world the way it is, and why can't we all just be good?

The answer starts with our willfulness. As we learned earlier, the Bible in Genesis shares how God told Adam and Eve they could eat all the fruit of the trees in the garden but warned them not to eat from one, the Tree of Knowledge of Good and Evil. For those not familiar with Christian teaching, this was not simply a piece of fruit, and it wasn't an arbitrary prohibition from God. It was intended to protect Adam and Eve from evil. And it was a test to see if they would obey him.

Up to that point in the creation story, Adam and Eve, the origin of humanity, knew God and were made in his image, and they enjoyed an intimate relationship with him. They knew only good, not evil, and they were free because God didn't make programmed robots. But they were tempted by the serpent, Satan, the embodiment of evil, who told them a lie that they could be as gods and that God just didn't want them to be equal to him. Of course, his lie ignores the fact that a created being can never be equal to its Creator. Yet Adam and Eve still believed the tempter instead of God. In much the same way, we believe politicians, scientists and many academics.

By eating the fruit, Adam and Eve took the knowledge of evil into their very being. Just as food becomes part of our bodies, evil became part of our nature. Ideas believed as truth enter our psyches, our souls, in disobedience to God. Christian doctrine calls this original sin because, at its very origin, humanity chose to disobey him and was poisoned with evil in mind, heart, body and soul. This is a spiritual fall from our state at creation. It is why we can't be exclusively good. Only through God's grace was any knowledge of good retained in us. This enabled humanity to exist without completely destroying itself.

Now, human beings experience both evil and pure desires. Impurity doesn't leave us just because we do good things and make wise choices. Everyone is capable of sin. No matter how many good choices we make in a row, the next one could be bad. The very fact that we have to choose between good and evil indicates there are bad desires within us. This knowledge doesn't leave our souls simply because we behave correctly most of the time.

We can no more remove evil from our being than we can extract food molecules from our bodies after we have eaten. Only God, our Maker, can eliminate evil from our being permanently. This is why

Jesus, the Son of God, was born: to save humanity. God needed a new, uncorrupted, sinless man for the salvation of the human race. This will be addressed further in Chapter 10, where we explore salvation. However, it is important to point out clearly for those who may still think all religions are the same: Christianity uniquely teaches that the complete removal of sin and reconciliation with God comes through divine grace alone—not through human effort or willpower. Other religions and philosophies place this burden on our ability to choose good over evil, right over wrong, and to transcend our desires altogether. This is a key difference. The disciplines of these religions or philosophies depend on the strength of the human will. Yet our self-discipline is imperfect, unstable and prone to failure. Only God can actually save.

Evil is always present in human nature even if it is ignored or not acted upon. However, given the right circumstances, or more accurately, the wrong circumstances, evil will be chosen. When people get angry or jealous enough, they can commit murder. If they are desperate enough, they lie, cheat and steal. When people lust after another badly enough, they commit adultery. If fear takes hold, we are capable of all kinds of atrocities. As the Milgram experiment shows, we will easily harm others if authorities tell us to.

That tipping point may be different in people who have a strong moral character versus a weak one, but we all have our breaking point where evil will come out. The difference between Christianity and other disciplines is that a Christian submits their will and life to God as their Savior, knowing they need God to remake them into his image and that they cannot do this by their own will.

Part Three. The Christian Worldview

CHAPTER 10

The Call of God

Having seen how false beliefs can shape worldviews and lead to destructive outcomes, it's worth turning now to the Christian perspective on truth and the purpose of belief itself. My hope is that this book helps you respond to God's call and discover the joy, peace and solid foundation he offers. God doesn't phone or email you. He calls each person inwardly, revealing himself deep within the heart—beyond words. We can choose to answer that call with a simple "yes."

Each religion makes its own claims about truth, and those must be considered within the context of that belief system. What follows is my best understanding of what is found in Christian teachings.

One unique feature of Christianity is that Jesus Christ was and is both God and man. This is how Christianity connects us with God's will and his ways. As will be explained later, it is God who accomplishes salvation for those who believe. This is not a casual or purely intellectual belief but a life-shaping truth rooted at the core of our being. This conviction in Jesus Christ as our Savior is our faith. It does not come through knowledge; it is a revelation in the soul of who he truly is.

Christians did not invent this truth. It is divine reality perceived and embraced—a conviction that calls forth the image of God still present in human nature. This belief recognizes our deep need for our Creator and our inability to save ourselves. As King David writes in Psalm 51:17, "The sacrifices of God are a broken spirit; a broken and contrite heart, O God, you will not despise." True faith begins when we stop rebelling and humbly accept his way instead of our own. He himself provided the way of salvation, and his name is Jesus Christ.

God became a man to reunite us to himself and to bridge the gap caused by humanity's rebellion and disobedience, which began with Adam and Eve. The Creator did not create multiple paths to salvation but one way, based on who Jesus Christ is and what he did, not on our good works. As discussed previously, all our right choices and behaviors cannot remove evil from our nature. Only God, our Maker, can remake us into his true image.

Jesus Christ, the Son of God and Son of Man, is a new starting point of humanity for those who believe. He is the new sinless Adam, as the apostle Paul teaches.

> Therefore, just as sin came into the world through one man [the original sin of Adam], and death through sin, and so death spread to all men because all sinned … But the free gift [of salvation] is not like the trespass. For if many died through one man's trespass, much more have the grace of God and the free gift [of salvation] by the grace of that one man Jesus Christ abounded for many [Jesus's sacrifice for our sin] (Romans 5:12, 15, words added).

This gift is for all who believe in Jesus for salvation. Through faith, we are united with Christ and with his sinless, righteous life as both the Son of God and the Son of Man. By that same faith, our sins are paid for through his sacrifice for us. In trusting Jesus, God removes evil from us—freeing us from sin in this life and on judgment day. This is the gospel of salvation, which is aptly named since *gospel* means "good news."

Right after John gives the gospel in a nutshell (John 3:16–17), he also offers a warning, a judgment in the next two verses.

> Whoever believes in him is not condemned, but whoever does not believe is condemned already, because he has not believed in the name of the only Son of God. And this is the judgment: the light has come into the world, and people loved the darkness rather than the light because their works were evil (John 3:18–19).

Evil became part of human nature when Adam and Eve disobeyed God's warnings and instructions and believed lies instead. Salvation comes from believing Jesus is our Savior in our core self and deciding to follow his will for our life. This is Christian faith. God is calling people through the gospel message. If you hear his call, then answer and believe.

CHAPTER 11

The Character of God

Christian theology is summarized in the Nicene Creed, which virtually all churches hold to be true. The creed is a condensed summary of Christian belief in God: the Father, Son and Holy Spirit. It is based on scriptures and early church teachings, and it was established at the First Council of Nicaea, AD 325 and was later refined at the First Council of Constantinople in AD 381. This creed summarizes the nature of God the Father and the purposes of God the Son and God the Holy Spirit. Here it is in full.

> I believe in one God, the Father almighty, maker of heaven and earth, and all that is, seen and unseen. I believe in one Lord, Jesus Christ, the only Son of God, eternally begotten of the Father, God from God, light from light, true God from true God, begotten, not made, of one being with the Father. Through him, all things were made. For us and for our salvation, he came down from heaven: by the power of the Holy Spirit he became incarnate from the Virgin Mary, and was made man. For our sake, he was crucified under Pontius Pilate; he suffered death and was buried. On the third day, He rose again in accordance with the Scriptures; he ascended into heaven and is seated at the right

hand of the Father. He will come again to judge the living and the dead, and his kingdom will have no end. I believe in the Holy Spirit, the Lord, the giver of life, who proceeds from the Father and the Son. With the Father and the Son he is worshipped and glorified. He has spoken through the prophets. I believe in one holy catholic and apostolic church,[91] and acknowledge one baptism for the forgiveness of sins. I look for the resurrection of the dead, and the life of the world to come. Amen.

The Nicene Creed faced the challenge of trying to describe God in words that are inherently limited. It seeks to explain the Creator, an eternal spirit unhindered by time or space, to beings bound by time and confined to three dimensions. God exists beyond the physical universe we know and experience. He is otherworldly, transcending the limits of human understanding and expression.

The foremost belief expressed in the creed is that there is only one God, not three, which is consistent with classical Christian teaching. But how can there be three persons: Father, Son and Holy Spirit? Again, God is different from us. Each one is eternal and exists separately from time. They simply are. They have the power of self-existence because they share one essence.

Some translations of the creed use the English word *substance* instead of *being*, but *substance* has a material connotation, and God is not made of material. But *being* is the best translation we have for the original Greek word *ousia*, which is the essence or very nature of something, an intangible, immaterial being.[92] The three persons are one, and only one, God because they all are of the

---

[91] The "catholic church" refers to the one universal church of believers, not the denomination of the Catholic church as we know it today. The "apostolic church" means it was founded by Jesus's apostles and the early church leaders taught by them.

[92] *Merriam-Webster Dictionary*, "ousia," accessed January 9, 2026, charlesmastroni.com/ousia.

same essence and nature of the same being—one that simply *is*. While they are distinct persons, they are perfectly one and in harmony with each other.

God existed before creation and, therefore, before time. Because he is outside of time, he is uncreated. Before creation, there was only God. Nothing else existed—no space, no matter, no time. The Nicene Creed tells us that the Father begot the Son, and the Holy Spirit proceeded from the Father and the Son. Since this happened before time began, the Son could only be of God, sharing the same being, or ousia, as the Father. The Father, Son and Holy Spirit are eternally one.

Even saying *begets* and *proceeds* suggests an element of time, which does not truly apply to God. These terms are concessions to our limited understanding. The three persons of the Trinity simply exist as one in perfect holiness, goodness and harmony, all-knowing and loving each other. Nothing is withheld between them. This is the source of love itself.

This unity creates a dynamo of power, will, knowledge, love and absolute perfection.[93] That is God, and he decided to create the universe and beings that can know him and share in existence. Christian teaching tells us this includes angels and human beings.

Yes, God is a completely different kind of being than we are, which should not be too big of a shock. And given our nature, this should also be a great comfort—God had better be superior to us, or where would we place our hope?

Creation as a Part of Foundational Knowledge

Out of God's boundless grace, he created beings that could know him as fully as possible and a good world for them to live in. As conscious beings with free will and made in his image, we get to share in the love the Trinity has for each part of itself and to reflect that into the world. Created beings are not God and never can be,

---

[93] Keller, *The Reason for God.*

but we can know and adore him for who he is and love each other in a similar way. If this knowledge shapes our being, we become very different people than without it. With it, we believe we owe our existence to God and that we need to live according to his objective morality. Without it, we are left shaped by the culture we live in, relying solely on its wisdom.

In the gospel of John, the Son of God, Jesus, is referred to as the Word. "In the beginning was the Word, and the Word was with God, and the Word was God. He was with God in the beginning. Through him all things were made; without him nothing was made that has been made" (John 1:1–3 NIV). As you can see, John's writings serve as a source for the Nicene Creed. Jesus, as the Word, is the very expression of God because he is God.

The book of Genesis explains that God spoke the Word, the Spirit moved, and the Trinity created the universe. Light and darkness, day and night, and the sun, moon and stars were made. Living things were also formed: plants, fish, birds and animals with the ability to procreate after their kind. Everything was created by God. Yet the crowning piece of his creation is Adam and Eve: humankind.

Christology

Thousands of books have been written trying to address Christology, which is a fancy word for the study of who Jesus Christ is. As the Nicene Creed tells us, Jesus is the Son, the second person in the Holy Trinity.

Jesus Christ was always the plan for the redemption of humanity if and when we failed to be true images of God. The first reference to the Son of God being born into this world is in Genesis when God punished the serpent, the spirit of evil, for corrupting humanity.

> The Lord God said to the serpent, "Because you
> have done this, cursed are you above all livestock

and above all beasts of the field; on your belly you shall go, and dust you shall eat all the days of your life. I will put enmity between you and the woman, and between your offspring and her offspring; he shall bruise your head, and you shall bruise his heel" (Genesis 3:14–15).

God curses Satan and crushes him through the offspring of the woman, Eve. God's created humanity is physical as well as spiritual, and evil needs to be conquered and punished on both these levels. This is why the Son of God also became the Son of Man, a name Jesus often used to refer to himself. The eventual offspring born of the woman is the Son of God, who entered the physical world as one of us. He was the perfect man, who came to conquer Satan (by crushing his head) and to suffer for humanity as one of us (by having his heel bruised). Jesus Christ is the only true hero of humankind. He saves us completely from evil in mind, body and spirit. As the apostle John states:

> And the Word became flesh and dwelt among us,
> and we have seen his glory, glory as of the only Son
> from the Father, full of grace and truth (John 1:14).

Jesus is fully God and fully human, united in one. Because of his unique being, he is the only one who can reunite people with God. No other religion makes this claim. Many times in the Gospels, Jesus clearly shows and even outright states he is the Son of God, the Messiah.

> So the Jews gathered around him and said to him, "How long will you keep us in suspense? If you are the Christ, tell us plainly." Jesus answered them, "I told you, and you do not believe. The works that I do in my Father's name bear witness about me, but you do not believe because you are not among my

> sheep. My sheep hear my voice, and I know them, and they follow me. I give them eternal life, and they will never perish, and no one will snatch them out of my hand. My Father, who has given them to me, is greater than all, and no one is able to snatch them out of the Father's hand. *I and the Father are one*" (John 10:24–30, emphasis added).

Many people believe Jesus was a great moral teacher who had a profound and lasting effect on the world, especially in Western culture, but they won't accept, and even deny, that Jesus of Nazareth as depicted in the Bible was also God who became man. The problem with this position is that Jesus does not permit it based on what he claimed about himself. Either he is right and he is the Son of God, or he is a nutcase with delusions of grandeur.

Jesus's life and works show him to be wise, good, moral and compassionate—the healer of thousands. In the Beatitudes (Matthew 5:1–12), he taught people to be meek, pure of heart, to seek righteousness, and to be peacemakers. He killed no one, cast out demons, and showed love to the poor, lame and sick. He forgave sinners. The only people Jesus was tough on were the hypocritical leaders he encountered, especially the religious ones. This is not the behavior of a nutcase egotist, yet he claims to be God incarnate.

By doing all these things, Jesus leaves no nice, comfortable middle ground for seeing him merely as a great teacher while denying that he is God made man. In his gospel, the apostle John witnessed Jesus making this claim. The Jewish people of their day knew what Jesus was asserting: that he himself was God. He knew what their reaction would be but still spoke clearly.

Jesus directly states, "I and the Father are one" (John 10:30) Here, the Father refers to God. The apostle John recorded many of Jesus's teachings. John shares these words from Jesus, spoken just hours before he was crucified for our sins:

Jesus said to him, "I am the way, and the truth, and the life. No one comes to the Father except through me. If you had known me, you would have known my Father also. From now on you do know him and have seen him."

Philip said to him, "Lord, show us the Father, and it is enough for us." Jesus said to him, "Have I been with you so long, and you still do not know me, Philip? Whoever has seen me has seen the Father. How can you say, 'Show us the Father'? Do you not believe that I am in the Father and the Father is in me? The words that I say to you I do not speak on my own authority, but the Father who dwells in me does his works. Believe me that I am in the Father and the Father is in me, or else believe on account of the works themselves" (John 14:6–11).

As God in the flesh, he knows us completely, for we too are both spirit and flesh, created by him. It is only because Jesus is both divine and human, perfect in each, that he can take away our sin. In Christ, God fully identifies with us, sharing our humanity while remaining wholly divine. This is why God becoming man is crucial: through Jesus, faithful believers are united with God himself. Since we are a unity of spirit and body, Jesus became a physical being as well, to redeem every part of us. As stated before, we cannot remove sin or the knowledge of evil from ourselves. At best, we can resist it, but only God can cleanse us completely.

No one except Jesus Christ can reunite us with God. It is like what the classic gospel song "Oh Happy Day" tells us: Jesus washed our sins away. True, complete salvation is deliverance from sin and death, and only God can totally remove sin from our psyche and give us eternal life. No one—not your parents, sibling, friend or lover—has done more to save you.

When we hear God's call and believe from our unique spiritual self, we are given faith in the promises of God. We trust in Jesus and in who he is. Faith accepts our need for a Savior and unites us with Christ.

An analogy that may help us understand this concept is the union of marriage. When we live closely with a spouse, we share life. We identify as husband and wife because we are actually part of each other physically and psychologically, and we are sharing experiences together in good times and bad. We are still two distinct people, but there is unity and love for each other and with each other, compatibility, and a oneness of mind, heart and body. There is true, intimate knowledge, understanding and love.

Accepting Christ, placing our faith in Jesus, is like that, but it happens deep within the soul. Since God took on flesh, Christ can bond with us, sharing our life with his and his life with each believer. Through this union, Jesus takes all our sin upon himself and bears the full weight of judgment in our place. God's wrath would destroy any ordinary person, but Jesus endured it for us. When he died carrying our sin, our sinful nature was put to death. In him, we are set free from God's wrath and condemnation.

Jesus was raised from the dead, so he even conquered the grave. (To learn more, refer to "Appendix 2: The Resurrection of Jesus Christ" on page 227). God expects those he saves to live holy, sinless lives. We don't do this perfectly, of course, but confession and forgiveness are now available to the faithful. "If we confess our sins, He is faithful and just to forgive us our sins and to cleanse us from all unrighteousness" (1 John 1:9). When the faithful believer is united with Jesus, they are also raised with him, freed from sin and made ready for eternity, spotless on the day of judgment.

> Whoever has my commandments and keeps them,
> he it is who loves me. And he who loves me will
> be loved by my Father, and I will love him and
> manifest myself to him. … If anyone loves me, he

> will keep my word, and my Father will love him,
> and we will come to him and make our home with
> him (John 14:21, 23).

Through the gift of faith, Christ unites with us. The Son of God and Son of Man takes our sin upon himself by claiming it as his own, even though he is sinless. Jesus then bears the wrath of God in place of the believing sinner. The Messiah gives us his sinless, righteous self because when we answer God's call and believe in our hearts, we become one with him.

Shortly before Jesus was arrested and crucified for our sins on the cross, he prayed this prayer for his disciples and all who would come to believe.

> I do not ask for these only, but also for those who
> will believe in me through their word, that they may
> all be one, just as you, Father, are in me, and I in
> you, that they also may be in us, so that the world
> may believe that you have sent me. The glory that
> you have given me I have given to them, that they
> may be one even as we are one, I in them and you
> in me, that they may become perfectly one, so that
> the world may know that you sent me and loved
> them even as you loved me. (John 17:20–23)

This saving work of Jesus was predicted in the Old Testament, over seven hundred years before Jesus's birth:

> But he was pierced for our transgressions; he
> was crushed for our iniquities; upon him was the
> chastisement that brought us peace, and with his
> wounds we are healed. All we like sheep have gone
> astray; we have turned—every one—to his own
> way; and the Lord has laid on him the iniquity of
> us all (Isaiah 53:5–6).

CHAPTER 12

The Essence of Humanity

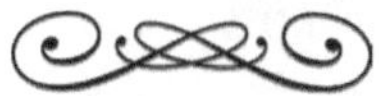

This brings us to the Christian teaching regarding humankind, our anthropology. God specially created men and women. We are not derived, nor have we evolved from the animal kingdom. Before the rebellion, we were his true images. Human beings are not God but are reflections of him, which separates us from the animals. We can know him in a way they can't since we can learn from him and about him. This makes it impossible for humanity to have evolved from apes. In Genesis 1:27, we previously saw we are not merely another part of the animal kingdom, as modern science would have us believe.

God wanted people to know him, love him and each other, and rule the earth under him as his reflection in it (Genesis 1:28). Classical Christian teaching states humanity is to live, marry and procreate within the marriage bond:

> So the Lord God caused a deep sleep to fall upon the man, and while he slept took one of his ribs and closed up its place with flesh. And the rib that the Lord God had taken from the man he made into a woman and brought her to the man. Then the man said, "This at last is bone of my bones and flesh of my flesh; she shall be called Woman, because she

> was taken out of Man." Therefore a man shall leave
> his father and his mother and hold fast to his wife,
> and they shall become one flesh (Genesis 2:21–24).

Man and woman are of the same essence, similar to the Trinity. Their rejoining is part of God's design. Male and female were separated so they could join and become one flesh again as husband and wife, to multiply and fill the earth. Heterosexual marriage has been the conduit of new life and the source of new people throughout history. This was God's design for humanity.

Only believers in modern progressivism contradict the fundamental truth that marriage is between a man and a woman (in other words, a biological male and a biological female). As previously mentioned, every culture in the history of humanity, from tribal cultures to sophisticated ones, has unquestionably accepted this definition of marriage.

As image-bearers of God, we are called to learn, discover and create good within the world he has entrusted to us, and we are supposed to do so responsibly, not wastefully. We should be good stewards of the blessing that is creation, but that does not mean we are to worship it.

Genesis 2:15 (NIV) says, "The Lord God took the man and put him in the Garden of Eden to work it and take care of it." As the Westminster Catechism teaches, "Man's chief and highest end is to glorify God, and fully to enjoy him for ever."[94] We are to use the abilities and gifts God gives us—intelligence, creativity and physicality—to bring glory to God as his children. We are to cooperate with his will and design, not work against him.

Consider what it means to be image-bearers of God. The rebellion of humanity did not destroy God's created images, even though it damaged or infected them. A body with an infection is still a body. Being his image-bearers means we retain knowing

---

[94] "Larger Catechism," *The Westminster Standard*, accessed January 9, 2026, charlesmastroni.com/westminster.

something of him, even though we have been tainted with the knowledge of evil as well.

Because God is creative, people are creative. Look at the great works of art that have been produced throughout history: paintings, literature, art, architecture and inventions. We can see the cleverness and ingenuity of people in all times and places, knowledge building upon knowledge over the centuries. Personally, I think God was tickled pink when we sent men to the moon. I can imagine him as a proud father telling the angels in heaven, "Look at what my kids are doing with what I gave them!"

Given that God is our Creator, he created every person who ever lived, including you and me. God, who brought this entire universe into being, thought it was a good idea to make you. You are not an accident. He intentionally designed you as a unique individual—both spirit and body. Even your one-of-a-kind set of fingerprints bears witness to your individuality.

Human beings are capable of great good or great evil with their God-given abilities. Some lean more toward one or the other, yet every one of us carries the potential for both. We see the good and noble side of humanity when natural disasters hit and people rescue those in need or when someone like Mother Teresa helps the poor. Even she recognized that God is essential. So what does that say about less-saintly individuals?

On the evil side, we see the rapists, child molesters and dictators of the world. Every human being is an imperfect image of God because of the knowledge of evil that has entered us. Consistently choosing good does not remove this knowledge—it only restrains it.

Everybody has value in God's eyes, including you, because his image is in you and he made you. God sees only one race, the human race. I wish more people thought that way. But this equality is why he commands us to help the poor and helpless.

As individuals made in God's image, we also retain an instinctive, inborn knowledge of paradise, our first environment.

All peoples and religions hope for a better place to live in and an improved, more perfect quality of life that is markedly different from their current one. Some people refer to their ideal world as enlightenment, while others call it nirvana, heaven or Zen. But we all know perfectly well that this world is not heaven.

The common qualities among these concepts of perfection are many: love without hate or envy, personal fulfillment without domination, genuine peace without war, justice without wickedness, health without disease, life without death. I could list more features, but you get the idea. John Lennon longed for this world and sang about it in "Imagine," but unfortunately, he denied God, who is the only one able to grant it.

As I previously mentioned, the Christian worldview is that Adam and Eve represent the origin of humanity. Science has cast doubt on this with genetics, evolutionary theory, the fossil record, and other interpretations of the natural world. However, science was not there at the creation of the world, nor were you or I. We are given an account of it in the Bible that is objective truth, not a set of scientific theories.

The Christian worldview is based on the Genesis account, which we believe was inspired by God and written by Moses. Through divine inspiration, he recorded the origins of the world and of humankind in a way that would convey timeless truth across every culture throughout history. Let's look at this reality in Christian anthropology from the book of Genesis.

Before the fall—before they rebelled and sinned—man and woman reflected the true image of God. Adam and Eve enjoyed a period of existence living in paradise, the Garden of Eden, as God made them, free to live within his design and will.

He did not want forced compliance from humanity but freely given love and obedience, so he gave them a chance to do so.

> And the Lord God commanded the man, "You are
> free to eat from any tree in the garden; but you

> must not eat from the tree of the knowledge of
> good and evil, for when you eat from it you will
> certainly die" (Genesis 2:16–17 NIV).

Adam and Eve knew God intimately and walked with him in Eden, filled with awe at his creation. They explored and delighted in all he had made for them. God knows what is good for his people and what is not. Living within his will is good, but Adam and Eve chose to go their own way instead.

God told them they were free to eat fruit from any tree they wanted, but he commanded them not to eat from one tree only, the one that would harm them. He warned them to avoid the knowledge of evil and the resulting consequences, but he did not force them to stop. People have the freedom to comply with the perfectly wise and good will of God or to decide what is right for themselves. They could choose to believe and obey his objective truth or disbelieve and disobey.

God wants genuine love, gratitude and willing obedience offered out of awe and respect for him. This cannot be forced, or we would be nothing more than robots. If our desire for him is to be true, it must come from our free will. Genuine love cannot be coerced, intimidated or bribed.

As stated previously, this is how perfect communion is expressed within the Trinity. God created us to share in it, but he desires our response to be freely given. Our purpose as bearers of his image is to receive what he offers, respond to him in devotion, and reflect his love into the world through how we live.

I feel compelled to respond to the question, "Why do bad things happen to good people?" The simple answer is that even after humanity consumed the knowledge of evil, God did not take away our freedom to choose. Yet now, people know how to do evil. Sin and rebellion have accumulated through the centuries as each generation continues to disobey God's design and morality. That is why bad things happen to good people. God does not cause evil—he cannot. Evil comes from human choices. And because he created us as free agents, he allows us to act as we choose.

We may wish it were different when terrible things happen to those we love, but God doesn't cause or condone suffering. He has granted us the gift of free will, although ultimately there will be punishment for those who commit terrible acts. However, in this fallen world, this is not guaranteed. This life is often unfair, yet God's heaven promises perfect justice and fairness. Bad things can happen to good people. The victims of sin may suffer without having done anything to deserve their fate. Take my cousin, for instance. He was driving safely and did nothing to attract the drunk driver who killed him and severely injured his wife. Illness, too, can strike anyone, regardless of their character.

What would a perfect world look like, where bad things didn't happen to good people? Evil and personal sin would not exist. You won't find pride or ego in heaven, but self-fulfillment is there. Christianity teaches true self-fulfillment is to become who and what God made you to be. The Bible describes heaven and hell in Revelation 21.

> Then I saw a new heaven and a new earth, for the first heaven and the first earth had passed away, and the sea was no more … And I heard a loud voice from the throne saying, "Behold, the dwelling place of God is with man. He will dwell with them, and they will be his people, and God himself will be with them as their God. He will wipe away every tear from their eyes, and death shall be no more, neither shall there be mourning, nor crying, nor pain anymore, for the former things have passed away."
>
> And he who was seated on the throne said, "Behold, I am making all things new." Also he said, "Write this down, for these words are trustworthy and true … But as for the cowardly, the faithless, the

> detestable, as for murderers, the sexually immoral,
> sorcerers, idolaters and all liars, their portion will
> be in the lake that burns with fire and sulfur, which
> is the second death" (Revelation 21:1, 3–5, 8).

This world is clearly not heaven, and it needs to be recreated without sin and disobedience. Humanity has not been able to create heaven on earth because the ills of this world were caused by our rebellion against God and the resulting sin.

God wants you and me and everyone else to have a good, loving and genuine relationship with him in faith and to accept his love, mercy and authority willingly. We are free to follow his way or not. Yet as Revelation tells us, at the end of our days, every person will be judged by God and given their due reward or punishment.

We can see the connection between the spiritual, invisible world of our thoughts and feelings and the physical world of our bodies when psychosomatic illnesses arise, which stem from what a person believes or thinks. Our psyche affects our physical self. Another example is the well-documented placebo effect, which is when an individual receives no medication but physically heals simply because they believe they have been treated. In the same way, someone who spends a long time dwelling on negative events establishes a pattern of thoughts, creating a chemical imbalance that leads to depression. Extreme cases of this can end in suicide, where destructive beliefs lead to death.

My point is that there is a connection between the invisible world and the physical one. And when humanity rebelled and took the knowledge of evil into themselves, they fell under its power. In time, both body and spirit were infected by it, so spiritual sickness resulted in physical maladies. This is why there are illnesses in this world. Choosing good and healthy thoughts over evil and unhealthy ones makes for a much better life individually and in our societies, but it doesn't guarantee evil will never touch us.

Some also ask, why then are there natural disasters, like hurricanes, floods, volcanoes and earthquakes? This one is harder for the modern mind to understand. However, in Genesis, humanity was the final crowning jewel of God's created world. We have dominion over the earth.

> Then God said, "Let us make man in our image, after our likeness. And let them have dominion over the fish of the sea and over the birds of the heavens and over the livestock *and over all the earth* and over every creeping thing that creeps on the earth" (Genesis 1:26, emphasis added).

When humanity became corrupted, nature did too. The apostle Paul states it this way:

> For I consider that the sufferings of this present time are not worth comparing with the glory that is to be revealed to us. For the creation waits with eager longing for the revealing of the sons of God. For the creation was subjected to futility, not willingly, but because of him who subjected it, *in hope that the creation itself will be set free from its bondage to corruption and obtain the freedom of the glory of the children of God.* For we know that the whole creation has been groaning together in the pains of childbirth until now (Romans 8:18–22, emphasis added).

God created everything, and nature is connected not only to him but also to humankind. It is not independent of either God or man. Just as the spiritual and physical are intertwined within us, the natural world is physically affected by our rebellion.

Spiritual disobedience against God's design has brought disorder into every level of creation, including the physical world. Because of this, suffering and imperfection touch both nature and humanity. Some people experience moral evil, such as violence that harms the innocent. Others face physical brokenness, such as birth defects or disease. For this reason, Christian teaching has always held that we live in a fallen, broken world.

But God created us for heaven, which we still desire. This is a remnant of his image, which remains in us, along with our ability to recognize what is good. And we long for this perfection of ourselves, others and the world.

The Limits of Human Wisdom

Even though we have a fallen nature, we forget that our knowledge and wisdom are limited. Instead, we think we are equal to God. We defend our viewpoints as fiercely as we cling to life itself. At our core, we are self-centered rather than God-centered. We form bonds with others who share our cultural backgrounds, identities and beliefs, seeking comfort in the familiar. It's easy for us to see what is wrong with everyone else but not so much with ourselves, especially because we surround ourselves with people who share the same values and worldview.

A group identity is essentially a collection of people who are like-minded. This is an expanded form of self-centeredness that reinforces and validates the beliefs of its members. From this mindset, individuals may judge and condemn those with different opinions or worldviews, often out of fear, insecurity, jealousy, revenge or hatred. And from such divisions, horrible things can result. Values and beliefs can differ significantly from one person, group, society and culture to the next. That is why we need God's objective truth to anchor us—to reveal what is right, constant and true beyond human perspective.

Christianity teaches humanity believes a lie that has become part of our nature—that we are equal to God. This leads to idolatry, man-made gods of all kinds. We want heaven on our terms, without God, and like those who built the Tower of Babel, we are convinced we can attain this. Look at today's idols: genetic engineering, AI, gender-affirming care, environmental activism, communist ideology, global governance, and distorted forms of social justice. All promise a utopia, a heaven, or some personal righteousness, but without God.

This same lie (that we can be equal to God) persuades us individually that we don't need him at all. We convince ourselves that we are capable of managing our lives free from his guidance. Our desire to live unencumbered by God's design permits us to create our own rules rather than submitting to his truth. We attempt to shape reality around what we want and prefer, crafting a version of heaven that exists only on our terms.

According to Genesis, the source of all that is true is God, who created all things to be good. Apart from him, we cannot obtain heaven. Only God's wisdom can perfectly determine what is objectively right. Man's discernment may begin with good intentions, but our sinful self-centeredness inevitably corrupts and twists it into something dangerous.

Every culture throughout history has established laws and rules to restrain sin. Yet no matter how good we try to be, we easily slip into wrongdoing when the right circumstances arise. Even with our best efforts, sin can surface in our thoughts and desires at any time, regardless of how carefully we try to hide it.

When we compare ourselves to other people, we come off looking pretty good, but this is not a true image of God. He is completely good; there is no evil in him. Only he can restore us to truly reflect who he is. The fact that we exist, yet did not create ourselves, should lead us to know, worship and praise the being who made us, our creator God. However, in our pride, we resist turning to him.

CHAPTER 13

The Source of Knowledge

In the Christian worldview, God is the source of all knowledge, part of which he shares with us. He created the entire universe and established the spiritual and physical properties that allow everything to work together in such a beautiful, complex and astounding way. God understands gravity, chemistry, physics, astrophysics, biology and every other field far more completely than any human ever could. Since we are made in his image, the knowledge we discover comes at the time and in the measure he chooses to reveal to us.

God also understands the human heart and mind with a depth far beyond our insight, and he knows precisely what a human being is meant to be. As bearers of his image, we have the capacity to glimpse the truth about both God and the world he made. We can use his creation to develop new ideas and inventions. Throughout history, humankind has made many discoveries (fire, tools, the wheel, language, agriculture, animal breeding, metalworking, mathematics, the sciences, electricity, medicine, flight and computers, to name just a few). Our minds retain the image of God, not as his equals, but as beings capable of learning, creating and shaping the physical world around us. Genesis teaches God gave humanity dominion over creation so we might use it wisely.

Yet history also shows this same capacity can be twisted toward evil, often in the name of doing good.

Knowledge existed before humanity because the ordered universe was formed before we were, and the one who possesses and applies it is God, the Creator of all things. If knowledge can be analogous to light, then humanity—as bearers of God's image—can receive and pass it on much like the moon reflects the light of the sun. The moon doesn't generate its own radiance. It shines because of what it receives from another source. In the same way, we do not originate the truth, but we can reflect true knowledge that comes from God. It is fitting, then, that we often use the word *reflection* to describe the act of thinking.

For humanity to believe we are the source of knowledge is like the moon believing it produces sunlight. I can think of no better definition of being a lunatic than this.

We also use the word *realize* when we learn something real, something true. Thus, we call it a real–ization. To realize a truth is to take knowledge into one's mind as part of oneself.

The most important realization is that God exists. The Bible describes him in many ways: Creator, Lord, Healer, all with the power of self-existence. He is perfectly holy, loving, just and merciful, and he wins in the end for his people. God is omniscient, all-powerful and sovereign.

Knowledge is discovered, not invented by humanity.

Man's theories are more from our pride and vanity.

In the Bible, God gives us essential knowledge.

And it differs from what they teach in college.

Whose mind is greater, the professor's or the Creator's?

CHAPTER 14

The Nature of Right and Wrong

Although we have been examining the TAKES elements of a worldview separately, they are all intertwined in our minds, hearts and spirits. Simply stated, the Christian view of ethics is and must be established by God. An objectively true morality is superior to any cultural system of morals, offering a clear definition of right and wrong.

Humanity may try to establish its own code of ethics, and successful long-lasting cultures do capture some objective morality, but so far, history has proven sustaining a moral framework based purely on human wisdom is impossible. Just as a partial truth mistaken for the whole truth is still a lie, partial morality mistaken as objective morality is amoral. Due to the knowledge of evil within every one of us, we cannot establish objective morality ourselves, since our nature is self-centered rather than God-centered.

On an individual level, the morality of a Christian should be motivated by a love of God and of their neighbor. Jesus summed up the Old Testament law with this statement when a Pharisee asked:

> "Teacher, which is the great commandment in the Law?" And he said to him, "You shall love the Lord your God with all your heart and with all your soul and with all your mind. This is the great

and first commandment. And a second is like it:
You shall love your neighbor as yourself. On these
two commandments depend all the Law and the
Prophets" (Matthew 22:36–40).

This is the proper motivation of a Christian. We certainly are not perfect, but genuine Christians strive to meet this standard because of their relationship with Jesus Christ. God- and neighbor-centered love is other-focused, the opposite of self-centered love. They are based on pleasing God by honoring his commandments because we have a loving relationship with him and know he is right.

Self-centered love produces an obedience that follows the rules simply to be seen as a good person in the eyes of the world and oneself. This type of compliance is ultimately self-serving and rooted in pride. While it can lead to a successful life measured by the world's standards and one's values, such so-called goodness is not aligned with God's objective morals and principles, because it doesn't flow from genuine belief or heartfelt obedience to the Creator.

Classical Christian teaching on the Old Testament law lists its three general uses:

1. **Civil:** to keep life peaceful between members of a community or nation by establishing right and wrong behavior between people and restraining and punishing sinful actions. This is part of God's grace to all peoples, so civilizations can last and societies can be livable. If murder, theft, adultery, cheating, corruption and the like are left unchecked, life becomes intolerable.

2. **Moral:** to show what God's will is for us. When the law confronts our harmful desires, it reveals the sin within us. We are not meant to indulge in those that conflict with the law. This realization can stir up fear of rejection or of being seen as a bad person. But ideally, it moves the Christian to recognize their need for God's grace, which forgives

and strengthens us to resist these desires. Scripture calls these "temptations." For example, when someone feels the urge to steal or commit adultery, they can obey the law for different reasons, either out of fear of condemnation or by turning to God for the strength to resist.

3. **Spiritual:** to reveal God's will and what he considers right and wrong. This goes beyond simply recognizing moral boundaries. It cultivates an awareness of God himself, which fuels our desire to be right with him and to please him, to honor our Maker and Savior, and to love others and be good to them.

In summary, the highest fulfillment of the law is obedience that flows from love for God and neighbor. A lesser form of it is doing what is right and resisting what is wrong simply because the moral code requires it. Lesser still is external obedience driven only by the desire to avoid punishment or other consequences. Sin, by contrast, is a self-centered and self-serving indulgence of temptation. It is an act of disobedience to God's will and a refusal to submit to his moral law.

CHAPTER 15

Our Deliverance from Sin

The best source for understanding the Christian worldview of salvation is the apostle John's description of it in Revelation 21:1, 3–8. There, he records the vision he received of God's final work at the end of days—an image he was commanded to write down.

Here is a summary of what John tells us about salvation:

- It restores us to a life with God, in his presence, as we were created originally (v. 1, 3).

- It saves us from all ills and suffering (v. 4).

- It ushers us into a new and perfected heaven and earth (v. 5).

- It is a gift from God, given without the need for repayment (v. 6).

- It will not be granted to everyone (v. 7).

- Those who reject salvation will be separated from God (v. 8).

Let's start by looking more closely at each of these verses.

In verse 1, John tells us about what he saw in his vision. "Then I saw a new heaven and a new earth, for the first heaven and the first earth had passed away, and the sea was no more." This recreation of heaven and earth will be our new eternal home, and it will be perfect because the sea of troubles present on this earth has passed away.

Verse 3 explains what happened next in the vision: "And I heard a loud voice from the throne saying, 'Behold, the dwelling place of God is with man. He will dwell with them, and they will be his people, and God himself will be with them as their God.'" God is announcing to us from his throne that we will live with him and enjoy his presence, the way we were always meant to. He will restore us to be his true images, and he will be present with us, sharing love, joy and goodness with each other and our neighbor.

Verse 4 reflects the deep love and compassion God has for his children. "He will wipe away every tear from their eyes, and death shall be no more, neither shall there be mourning, nor crying, nor pain anymore, for the former things have passed away." God will grant us salvation from death, sickness, pain and suffering because this fallen world is no more. He can and will make all things right again.

Verse 5 contains a promise to humanity and God's instruction to John to ensure we hear his vow. "And he who was seated on the throne said, 'Behold, I am making all things new.' Also he said, 'Write this down, for these words are trustworthy and true.'" God will make a new world without sin in it. When he had finished creation, we are told in Genesis (the first book of the Bible), "And God saw everything that he had made, and behold, it was very good" (Genesis 1:31). When God remakes creation, as promised in Revelation (the last book of the Bible), it will also be very good.

Verse 6 reveals God has rescued us from death and will usher us into his presence. "And he said to me, 'It is done! I am the Alpha and the Omega, the beginning and the end. To the thirsty I will give from the spring of the water of life without payment.'" God is the giver of life, and the salvation he offers is described as "life-giving water," which represents the salvation he provides. Jesus paid the price for our wrongdoing when he died on the cross, and because of his sacrifice, our sins are forgiven and we are spared from having to pay the penalty they deserve, which is death.

Verse 7 identifies those who will be adopted into his family as his children. "The one who conquers will have this heritage, and I will be his God and he will be my son." By faith, we must conquer our pride and repent, accepting the needed salvation offered by Jesus Christ. Faith is a gift from God, a revelation that is shown to us, believed and followed. Finding the courage to accept this belief is also a gift of grace given by the Holy Spirit. No sinful people are in God's final heaven because all who gain salvation are also saved from their sin.

In verse 8, we learn those who are not redeemed and who remain faithless, continuing in their evil way of life, will not be saved into God's final heaven and earth. "But as for the cowardly, the faithless, the detestable, as for murderers, the sexually immoral, sorcerers, idolaters and all liars, their portion will be in the lake that burns with fire and sulfur, which is the second death." Yet those who trust in Christ and receive God's gifts of faith, mercy and righteousness will inherit a perfect world and live among sinless people, restored as true and unspoiled images of God. For the faithful, our iniquity has already been judged and punished in Jesus Christ. But all who persist in their sin will face judgment and be sent to hell, a place that is the opposite of God's new heaven and earth.

Let's unpack the meaning of these various aspects of salvation.

Salvation from Sin

The first aspect of salvation in Jesus Christ is deliverance from our sinful nature through atonement. This act can be thought of as seeking "at-one-ment" or unity with God. Because he is perfectly holy and just, we cannot be united to him without our sin being paid for. Jesus made that payment in full, and through faith in him, we are reconciled to God.

This is no "cheap grace." Jesus suffered in our place, and our salvation requires sincere repentance from us in acknowledgment of our need for him. Repentance is a 180-degree turn from ignoring God and pretending we do not need him to knowing that we are lost without him. J. I. Packer gives a clear definition of repentance.

> Repentance means turning from as much as you know of your sin to give as much as you know of yourself to as much as you know of your God, and as our knowledge grows at these three points so our practice of repentance has to be enlarged.[95]

Repentance is not a one-time event. It is an ongoing part of the Christian life. Yet this practice is often lacking among those people who profess to follow Christ. True repentance means seeing our sin clearly and admitting the evil desires that caused it. We must confess our defiance of God and recognize we are sinners in need of his mercy. In response, God grants the grace of forgiveness. But he is never fooled by insincere repentance.

Salvation begins when we answer God's call—repenting and accepting the gifts of faith, mercy and righteousness offered in Jesus. Faith unites us with him, creating a life rooted in Christ. As noted earlier in "Christology" (on page 186), this union means we share his life and identity. In other words, we are joined to him in a profound spiritual oneness.

Because Jesus is both God and man, he can take our sinful nature into himself and impart his righteousness to us. We are crucified with him on the cross because we are united with him. As the apostle Paul writes, "We know that our old self was crucified with him in order that the body of sin might be brought to nothing, so that we would no longer be enslaved to sin" (Romans 6:6).

---

[95] J. I. Packer, *Keep in Step with the Spirit: Finding Fullness In Our Walk With God,* second edition (Intervarsity Press, 2020).

Just before that, Paul addressed our ongoing struggle with sin, even after we are saved. Aware of our human weakness, he challenged believers by asking:

> What shall we say then? Are we to continue in sin that grace may abound? By no means! How can we who died to sin still live in it? Do you not know that all of us who have been baptized into Jesus Christ were baptized into his death? We were buried therefore with him by baptism into death, in order that, just as Christ was raised from the dead by the glory of the Father, we too might walk in newness of life. For if we have been united with him in a death like his, we shall certainly be united with him in a resurrection like his (Romans 6:1–5).

Faithful believers have full unity with Christ and all the benefits of Jesus's saving work, including the gift of new life. Yet Paul reminds us that our transformation will not be finished until the end of our days. We still live in our physical bodies, and the old habits and passions remain in us until we die. This is why believing Christians can and do still sin.

However, through faith and our union with Christ, we have a new life that defeats old ingrained behaviors and desires. We are called to turn from sin and pursue righteousness. This walk of faith is a continual struggle between the new life and the old self, but Christians are to walk this path of victory—conquering sin instead of indulging it. When we fail, we repent, confess and are forgiven. We then stand again and continue walking toward Christ.

Paul then concludes this topic by describing how we are to live as Christians, united to Christ but still bound by time.

> Let not sin therefore reign in your mortal body, to make you obey its passions. Do not present your members to sin as instruments for unrighteousness,

> but present yourselves to God as those who have
> been brought from death to life, and your members
> to God as instruments for righteousness. For sin
> will have no dominion over you, since you are not
> under law but under grace (Romans 6:12–14).

Every time we face temptation, God gives the faithful believer the strength to overcome it and to walk in obedience through his grace. In this changed life, our free will is empowered by love and gratitude toward the God who saved us. Paul reminds Christians of this truth in a letter to another church.

> No temptation has overtaken you that is not
> common to man. God is faithful, and He will
> not let you be tempted beyond your ability; but
> with the temptation He will also provide the
> way of escape, that you may be able to endure
> it (1 Corinthians 10:13).

This is the ongoing work of grace within salvation. God's power enables us to resist sin and live faithfully even as we still walk this earth.

We are not made instantly holy when we come to faith in Christ, but our sin is forgiven and the direction of our lives shifts toward holiness and a sincere, willing obedience to God. Christians still stumble, yet failure is not the end. We trust him, learn from our mistakes, and grow over time. Through faith, we experience the truth of Jesus and all he has done for us. God is now our ally, and in unity with Christ, we want to obey him. When we do, we find:

- peace with God and ourselves.

- the person our Creator made us to be.

- meaning and our true purpose in life.

We cannot be our genuine selves without knowing and loving our Maker and being in awe of him. He is at the center of everything—not you, me or any other person, except Jesus, who is both God and man. When we recognize this, we become God-centered instead of remaining self-centered.

Most of us think we deserve salvation—but do we? Even by our own cultural standards, we all sin. Have you ever lied, cheated, denied God, envied someone, or taken something that wasn't yours? And what about the acts most cultures deem to be far worse: murder, rape, adultery, abuse?

If you insist you have no sin, consider this: what if every thought and feeling you had for an entire week were made public? I'm talking about every one of them—about your parents, spouse, boss, coworkers, children, enemies or even friends. What if everyone knew how you felt about them? What about the thoughts you harbor toward those who have angered or offended you? Whether we act on them or not, these desires exist within every human heart. And God knows each of them and still loves us.

Cultural laws and standards rightly condemn the worst behavior through punishment or imprisonment. And it is beneficial that most people adhere to these standards. But this moral awareness—the knowledge of good—does not eliminate the evil still residing in us. We were created to be true, unspoiled images of God, and only he, through Jesus Christ, can make us so.

Salvation into God's Family

Where do you belong for eternity? In the Christian worldview, salvation also means you are part of God's family. Jesus is your brother, God is your father, and you have the Holy Spirit living in you. You are one with the Holy Trinity. You have a multitude of brothers and sisters, all of whom are redeemed through Jesus Christ. Revelation says:

> After this I looked, and behold, a great multitude
> that no one could number, from every nation,
> from all tribes and peoples and languages, standing
> before the throne and before the Lamb, clothed in
> white robes, with palm branches in their hands, and
> crying out with a loud voice, "Salvation belongs to
> our God who sits on the throne, and to the Lamb!"
> (Revelation 7:9–10)

"The Lamb" here refers to Jesus, described many times in the Bible as the Lamb of God who takes away the sin of the world.

God plans on saving a very large family. Are you part of it? You can be through faith in Jesus Christ.

Salvation from Death to Eternal Life

We all have a big problem—we die. Do you have a solution for this? God does. Our bodies will eventually cease to be alive, but we are not just physical beings. The person inside the body lives on. If our individual selves, traditionally referred to as our soul or spirit, continue after death, then what is our eternal fate?

Everyone dies. Even Jesus died in order to pay for our sins and to conquer death for us. The Bible does have two examples of individuals taken up to God bodily without physically dying first: Enoch and Elijah. Even so, their presence in this world ended. Unless you expect to be like them, your life will end. Then what?

Some philosophers and materialists argue we simply cease to be when our bodies die. But do we truly stop existing? Does our invisible internal self, with all of its thoughts, feelings and memories, just vanish? If the materialists are right, then every person's life would ultimately be meaningless.

Many people believe they will see their life pass before them when they die. What will you see? If you no longer exist and are kaput, what would be the motivation to live a good life versus an evil one?

Jesus states the issue this way: "For what does it profit a man to gain the whole world and forfeit his soul?" (Mark 8:36) Even if everyone loved or respected us, it would mean nothing if our souls did not live on. Without the soul's existence beyond death, life itself loses its ultimate meaning.

But I say the materialists are wrong. There must be life after death because of the very nature of time and eternity, which is not the extension of time—it exists beyond time altogether. To use a spatial analogy, eternity encompasses all of time and existence. Everything that happens does so within it. Perhaps it's better said that the essence of eternity is existence itself, or that the passage of time is woven into its fabric. Therefore, if anything exists at all, it does so within eternity, even if only for a moment. That means you and I continue to exist after we die, because we are more than our bodies. Our thoughts exist, so they will survive in eternity. Our memories exist, so they remain in eternity. Our love and hate exist, so they too endure in eternity.

This truth applies to every event in recorded history, from the smallest to the greatest. Since your life and mine take place within time, they also rest on an eternal foundation. History may not see us as famous, but it is composed of countless moments and the lives of everyday people woven together in time.

A great example of the workings of the fabric of time was in the movie *Back to the Future*. When Marty McFly interferes with the past, it seems as if his parents will no longer meet at the Enchantment Under the Sea dance. As Marty looks at a photo, he slowly disappears from the picture. Since his mom and dad never met, he would never be born.[96] Yet once a person exists, they become part of eternity. Do you think of yourself as being eternal?

---

[96] "Marty at the Enchantment Under the Sea Dance," *Back to the Future,* directed by Robert Zemeckis (1985).

Objectively, history is everything that has ever happened, whether great or small, recorded or not. Every breath you have ever taken is part of it. If it weren't, you wouldn't be alive right now. This is history on both a grand and personal scale. You are real, and everything that has happened to you and will happen to you—everything you did and will do—is part of history. You are eternally real, and so is everything you are and everything you do. That is a true legacy, not merely a memory.

If we do not cease to exist when our bodies die, what is our eternal fate? The answer certainly must involve both salvation to a great eternal destiny and salvation *from* a horrible one.

Salvation from a Broken World to Heaven

Deliverance from a terrible eternal fate is at the heart of God's work of salvation. After all, what would be the point of living forever in this broken world with a sinful self in a deteriorating body? Salvation must offer something far greater, including a heaven free from sickness, evil, death and decay.

We need salvation from our sin-infected hearts. Otherwise, our eternal life would be nothing more than a continuation of the same struggles we face now. Unless we, and the world itself, are made sinless, history will only repeat itself, along with each of our personal failures. Salvation offers a completely new life, untouched by evil or the darker sides of human nature. This perfection is a defining quality of heaven. We can imagine such a place, but we cannot reach it without God.

CHAPTER 16

A Final Word

Yes, salvation is wonderfully good. Judgment is completely perfect and justified. The Father has delegated authority to Jesus "to judge the living and the dead," as affirmed in the Nicene Creed. There is no better judge than God, who became man and experienced temptation and hardship, love and friendship, betrayal and suffering. Condemnation is a real possibility for our eternal fate, because evil must be eliminated from a saved world and a saved people. If it is not, then this present world will simply be repeated.

When God created the universe, everything in it was very good, including humanity. At the end of time, he is victorious and gets what he wants: a world that is good and people who are his true images. Salvation is the work of Jesus Christ. He redeems creation for those who have faith in him and submit to him as the one who saves us. Those who continue to deny him in their hearts and minds will not enter God's new heaven and earth. Christ judges, rules and decides who he will allow into his kingdom. This is not our choice, but his.

God provides the way of salvation to all who will answer his call and repent, turning 180 degrees from a self-centered life toward a God-centered one. As Jesus said at the beginning of his earthly ministry, "Repent, for the kingdom of heaven is at hand" (Matthew 4:17).

God is perfectly holy and cannot tolerate sin. He is also love, and he loves so purely that he cannot forever let evil destroy the work of his hands. He made human beings free to know, love and obey him and his objective truth. As a result, people may choose to reject him or believe their own ideas of right and wrong. However, sin is destructive, a cancer in humanity and in the world at large. God is the Creator and Healer. He has provided the way of salvation for us in Jesus Christ. God cannot abide rebellion in the new and final heaven and earth. He forbears with our present sinfulness and withholds his wrath so many can be saved when they repent of their sin and accept the gift of salvation through Jesus Christ.

God's wrath will destroy sin. For those who are saved in Jesus Christ, that wrath has already been satisfied—Jesus took upon himself the punishment we deserved. Through his sacrifice, our sin was destroyed when we were united with him. As previously mentioned, the prophet Isaiah foretold he would do this seven hundred years before Jesus lived (Isaiah 53:5–6). There is judgment for every person who ever lived or who will live. We may not like it, but it is so. We can be judged by God standing on our own merits or be saved by Jesus Christ and the work he did for us.

Ultimately, God gets to decide who enters his eternal kingdom, and Jesus is the perfect judge since he is fully God and fully human. Jesus said of himself, "I am the way, the truth and the life. No one comes to the Father except through me" (John 14:6). He also said, "My sheep hear my voice, and I know them, and they follow me" (John 10:27). Will you hear God's call and answer it, or will you continue to dismiss it and put it off?

If we live a life without God, touting our record of good behavior will not get us into heaven, no matter how good a life we may have lived according to our cultural standards or our own understanding. To accomplish our salvation, God must remake us, which requires a relationship with Jesus and submission to his will and his ways.

Yet our human nature shakes its fist at God and declares without hesitation, "Why can't God just accept me as I am? Why do I have to submit to him?" Satan convinced Adam and Eve of the same lie of arrogance. And humanity still stubbornly believes they can discern good from evil just as well as God can. The liar said, "For God knows that when you eat of it your eyes will be opened, and you will be like God, knowing good and evil" (Genesis 3:5).

Many people think God has no right to judge us, but he does. This lie started in the garden with the king of liars. Jesus described the devil while telling his accusers:

> You are of your father the devil, and your will is to do your father's desires. He was a murderer from the beginning, and does not stand in the truth, because there is no truth in him. When he lies, he speaks out of his own character, for he is a liar and the father of lies (John 8:44).

We did not call the universe into being, nor did Adam and Eve or the devil. Did you or I create ourselves? No. Are you or I the source of objective good, objective right, objective truth, or objective love? No. All these belong to God—only he possesses perfect justice, mercy, wisdom, omniscience and omnipotence. We owe our lives to him, and if he calls you or me to salvation, that is also his choice. We can submit to God, putting aside our pride, or we can continue rejecting him. Your eternal fate and mine hinge on God's graciousness, calling us back to himself. I pray you will answer his call.

Jesus said, "Behold, I stand at the door and knock. If anyone hears my voice and opens the door, I will come in to him and eat with him, and he with me" (Revelation 3:20). I suggest you answer the door!

Thank you for reading *Why Not God?* If you've enjoyed reading this book, please leave a review on your favorite review site. In doing so, you may help a soul to know the Lord and his salvation, which brings peace and wisdom for living in this world and the next.

APPENDIX 1

The Virgin Birth

The virgin birth can be another stumbling block for many people. In the Christian worldview, God is the Creator of life. Therefore, he could easily create a life without the necessity of sexual intercourse. The gospel writer Luke makes it plain this is not the same as the pagan gods of the Greeks and Romans, because they routinely took human form to enjoy the lustful pleasure of sex. Luke was familiar with the antics of these gods. By the time he was alive, both the Greeks (under Alexander the Great) and the Romans had conquered and occupied the lands of Judah and Israel.

Luke's description clarifies there was no sexual contact with Mary. God, who created life in the beginning, created a new life in Mary without taking human form or having sex, and Mary remained a virgin when Jesus's human form was conceived.

> In the sixth month the angel Gabriel was sent from God to a city of Galilee named Nazareth, to a virgin betrothed to a man whose name was Joseph, of the house of David. And the virgin's name was Mary. And he came to her and said, "Greetings, O favored one, the Lord is with you!" But she was greatly troubled at the saying, and tried

to discern what sort of greeting this might be. And the angel said to her, "Do not be afraid, Mary, for you have found favor with God. And behold, you will conceive in your womb and bear a son, and you shall call his name Jesus. He will be great and will be called the Son of the Most High. And the Lord God will give to him the throne of his father David, and he will reign over the house of Jacob forever, and of his kingdom there will be no end."

And Mary said to the angel, "How will this be, since I am a virgin?"

And the angel answered her, "The Holy Spirit will come upon you, and the power of the Most High will overshadow you; therefore the child to be born will be called holy—the Son of God" (Luke 1:26–35).

The power of the Most High created life in the Virgin Mary, as it was foretold. "Therefore the Lord himself will give you a sign. Behold, the virgin shall conceive and bear a son, and shall call his name Immanuel" (Isaiah 7:14). Critics often claim that the Hebrew word for *virgin* in this verse (*'almah*) can be translated as a young woman or maiden (a girl of marriageable age), rather than the technical term for virgin (*betulah*).[97] However, the prophet Isaiah claimed this was a sign that was out of the ordinary. Hebrew boys certainly seduced some Hebrew girls, who eventually bore children. That would not be a significant sign from God. Therefore, to be miraculous, Isaiah clearly means an actual virgin will bear a son without having sexual intercourse. A true virgin birth is the only reason this would be any kind of sign.

---

[97] Hallvard Hagelia, "Almah in Isaiah 7:14," *The Bible and Interpretation,* April 2012, charlesmastroni.com/almah.

The bigger question is, why did God do this? At its origin, humanity was infected with sin because of our disobedience to God, the belief we are equal to him, and the knowledge of evil in us. With the virgin birth of Jesus, God created a new starting point for humanity: a new man, one that is sinless in spirit and body.

God also calls us to be sinless, because that is how he created us. As stated in Chapter 15, his goal is to restore a new, sinless humanity through Jesus, who is the new beginning of this renewed creation. By becoming human, the Son of God made it possible for us to be united with him and reunited with God.

The Resurrection of Jesus Christ

The Christian belief that Jesus Christ died on the cross and rose from the dead is a stumbling block for many. As modern, educated people, we tend to doubt those ancient accounts in light of our current medical understanding. Some suggest that Jesus wasn't really dead, that he was only unconscious or in a coma. Yet, there is clear evidence he actually died and rose from the dead. These days, we expect video footage or scientific proof, but of course, that isn't possible from the time of Christ. What we do have, however, are multiple eyewitness accounts and the plain reasoning of common sense.

Did Jesus actually die? Yes. The Romans were expert executioners. Jesus was brutally beaten and whipped, suffering severe blood loss, as did all those they crucified. Crucifixion was particularly cruel. Weakened by the beatings, with hands and feet nailed or bound to the cross, the crucified would slowly suffocate as their own body weight pulled against their arms and compressed their chest, making it nearly impossible to breathe. To take each breath, they had to push upward painfully with their feet and pull with their arms. They hung there naked for all to see as a lesson to any who defied Rome. Victims were never taken down until they were unquestionably dead.

The Roman soldiers carried out their orders diligently. Death was common in those days, and people knew it when they saw it. They died in childbirth and from diseases and infections modern medicine now prevents. According to the eyewitness accounts of the apostles, Jesus was later stabbed in the side with a spear—a method the Romans had mastered to ensure a victim's death. Common sense tells us he was truly dead when he was taken down from the cross and laid in a tomb, which was sealed with a massive stone. Roman soldiers also guarded Jesus's burial place to prevent his followers from removing the body. The idea that a man so brutally beaten could somehow awaken from a coma, roll away the stone, and overpower trained guards defies logic. This is compelling evidence, and it is a rather fanciful speculation to think Jesus did not die.

The Bible also addresses the claim Jesus's body was stolen—a theory often presented as a rational explanation for the empty tomb on Easter morning. Once it was discovered that Jesus was no longer in the tomb, common sense tells us they would have searched for the body. And if it had been hidden anywhere, the Romans would have found it, given their brutal interrogation techniques. The fact that they didn't provides significant evidence supporting the resurrection. After all, if Jesus truly rose from the dead, as Christians throughout history have believed, that event was supernatural by nature and beyond human explanation.

The Easter story is recounted in Matthew, written by one of Jesus's disciples who witnessed the events:

> Now after the Sabbath, toward the dawn of the first day of the week, Mary Magdalene and the other Mary went to see the tomb. And behold, there was a great earthquake, for an angel of the Lord descended from heaven and came and rolled back the stone and sat on it. His appearance was like lightning, and his clothing white as snow. And

for fear of him the guards trembled and became like dead men. But the angel said to the women, "Do not be afraid, for I know that you seek Jesus who was crucified. He is not here, for he has risen, as he said. Come, see the place where he lay. Then go quickly and tell his disciples that he has risen from the dead, and behold, he is going before you to Galilee; there you will see him. See, I have told you." So they departed quickly from the tomb with fear and great joy, and ran to tell his disciples. And behold, Jesus met them and said, "Greetings!" And they came up and took hold of his feet and worshipped him. Then Jesus said to them, "Do not be afraid; go and tell my brothers to go to Galilee, and there they will see me."

While they were going, behold, some of the guard went into the city and told the chief priests all that had taken place. And when they had assembled with the elders and taken counsel, they gave a sufficient sum of money to the soldiers and said, "Tell people, 'His disciples came by night and stole him away while we were asleep.' And if this comes to the governor's ears, we will satisfy him and keep you out of trouble." So they took the money and did as they were directed. And this story has been spread among the Jews to this day (Matthew 28:1–15).

If we accept Jesus was truly dead when he was laid in the tomb, given that resurrection is a supernatural act, Matthew's account is a much more likely scenario than any ruse by Jesus's followers. How would they overcome a contingent of Roman guards? And how would they roll away a huge stone without waking them if they had fallen asleep?

Was Jesus Christ truly risen from the dead? Yes. The eyewitness testimonies of the apostles and the two Marys in the passage above attest to it. In addition, Jesus appeared to his disciples and hundreds more of his followers over a period of forty days after his death. Were they all liars, fools or delusional? The apostle Paul addresses this very question in his first letter to the church in Corinth, responding to those who were doubting his previous teachings.

> Now I would remind you, brothers, of the gospel I preached to you, which you received, in which you stand, and by which you are being saved, if you hold fast to the word I preached to you—unless you believed in vain.
>
> For I delivered to you as of first importance what I also received: that Christ died for our sins under the Scriptures, that he was buried, that he was raised on the third day under the Scriptures, and that he appeared to Cephas [the apostle Peter's Hebrew name], then to the twelve [disciples]. *Then he appeared to more than five hundred brothers at one time,* most of whom are still alive, though some have fallen asleep. Then he appeared to James, then to all the apostles (1 Corinthians 15:1–7, words and emphasis added).

Scholars date this letter to around AD 54, twenty-one years after Jesus's death and resurrection. At that time, all the apostles were preaching the same central message—that Jesus died for our sins and rose from the dead. Paul challenged anyone who doubted the truth to verify it with the five hundred witnesses who saw the resurrected Christ. Essentially, he was telling doubters: "Write to them, send messengers to them, and ask them if you do not believe it." Many of the eyewitnesses were still alive, offering overwhelming testimony to Jesus's resurrection from death to new life.

Could a false conspiracy really endure for two thousand years? Would so many people lie about it and willingly die for it? The early church faced relentless oppression. Believers were executed for refusing to worship the Caesars as gods. From the inception of Christianity, the Jewish synagogues also opposed them throughout the Roman world. With minor respites, the church endured persecution for its first three hundred years, all because of the testimony and teachings of the apostles and the early writings of Scripture, as noted in Chapter 4.

Would people hold to these beliefs if they weren't true, especially when doing so meant persecution and death? Why would anyone risk their life for a lie? The apostles and early church fathers gained no wealth or earthly benefit by proclaiming their faith. Their message brought suffering, not comfort, yet they remained steadfast because they had witnessed the truth.

All four gospel writers wrote of Jesus's death and resurrection. Could all of this really be an elaborate scheme meant to fool the world? What would be the point of sticking to a story so difficult for the natural mind to comprehend?

In the gospel of John, Jesus appears to the disciples after his resurrection and speaks with the apostle Thomas, who had been absent during Jesus's earlier visit to the disciples. To prove Jesus truly had risen from the dead, he says to Thomas:

> "Put your finger here, and see my hands; and put out your hand, and place it in my side. Do not disbelieve, but believe." Thomas answered him, "My Lord and my God!" Jesus said to him, "Have you believed because you have seen me? Blessed are those who have not seen and yet have believed" (John 20:27–29).

Jesus told Thomas to do these shocking things so he would believe. The apostle John witnessed and recorded this exchange so future generations would know what happened.

The gospel of Luke records another encounter with the risen Christ. Two of Jesus's followers were leaving Jerusalem in grief and sorrow to travel to Emmaus. They encountered Jesus and eventually returned to Jerusalem to tell the remaining eleven disciples. (Judas had committed suicide after he betrayed Jesus.)

> And they rose that same hour and returned to Jerusalem. And they found the eleven, and those who were with them gathered together, saying, "The Lord has risen indeed, and has appeared to Simon!" Then they told what had happened on the road, and how he was known to them in the breaking of the bread.

> As they were talking about these things, Jesus himself stood among them, and said to them, "Peace to you!" But they were startled and frightened and thought they saw a spirit. And he said to them, "Why are you troubled, and why do doubts arise in your hearts? See my hands and my feet, that it is I myself. Touch me, and see. For a spirit does not have flesh and bones as you see that I have." And when he had said this, he showed them his hands and his feet. And while they still disbelieved for joy and were marveling, he said to them, "Have you anything here to eat?" They gave him a piece of broiled fish, and he took it and ate before them.

> Then he said to them, "These are my words that I spoke to you while I was still with you, that everything written about me in the Law of Moses

> and the Prophets and the Psalms must be fulfilled."
> Then he opened their minds to understand the
> Scriptures, and said to them, "Thus it is written,
> that the Christ should suffer and on the third day
> rise from the dead, and that repentance for the
> forgiveness of sins should be proclaimed in his
> name to all nations, beginning from Jerusalem. You
> are witnesses of these things" (Luke 24:33–48).

The risen Jesus ate food, and those who were present touched him—this was no ghost or spirit. He told them to witness these things, so we have a record of these events written in the Bible for all generations as evidence of God's plan of salvation through Jesus Christ, the Son of God and the Son of Man, who died for our sins and rose again.

I ask you: if God is the Creator of the world and of life itself, as Christianity teaches, why is it so hard to believe Jesus died and rose again? After all, his resurrection is the perfect physical demonstration of God's plan of salvation—his proof of eternal life. We cannot conquer death, but God can, because he is the living Creator. And he raised his Son from the dead. Jesus is the new Adam, resurrected to conquer death for all who are being saved. He was resurrected to bring salvation and the promise of eternal life.

After he rose from the dead, he ascended into heaven. Eyewitnesses testified to this and recorded it for all generations.

> So when they had come together, they asked him,
> "Lord, will you at this time restore the kingdom
> to Israel?" He said to them, "It is not for you to
> know times or seasons that the Father has fixed by
> his own authority. But you will receive power when
> the Holy Spirit has come upon you, and you will
> be my witnesses in Jerusalem and in all Judea and

Samaria, and to the end of the earth." And when he had said these things, as they were looking on, he was lifted up, and a cloud took him out of their sight. And while they were gazing into heaven as he went, behold, two men stood by them in white robes, and said, "Men of Galilee, why do you stand looking into heaven? This Jesus, who was taken up from you into heaven, will come in the same way as you saw him go into heaven" (Acts 1:6–11).

Acknowledgments

I want to thank the many members of The Sherman Church who encouraged my preaching over the years. Their support and feedback gave me the idea that I might be able to write a book to serve the Lord.

And I want to thank my publisher, Emerald Lake Books, and my editor Tara R. Alemany, whose expertise and input were much needed by a first-time author to produce a quality book worth reading.

About the Author

Charles Mastroni is a lifelong learner who brings both practical experience and spiritual insight to his writing and preaching. After earning his bachelor's degree from Pennsylvania State University, he began a fifteen-year career working in global sourcing and purchasing, during which he also earned an MBA from Western Connecticut State University. Earlier in his career, he was a self-employed tradesman and foreman in construction—work that taught him the value of integrity, diligence and building on a solid foundation.

In 1989, after leaving behind the turbulence of the 1970s, Charlie turned to God in search of meaning and found the life-changing faith that now shapes his worldview. He continues to study Scripture and deepen his faith. Charlie previously attended classes at Reformed Theological Seminary and now teaches and guest preaches regularly in his local church, where he also serves as deacon emeritus.

Charlie lives in Connecticut and remains close with his two grown children. When he's not studying or writing, he enjoys following his favorite sports—especially American football, basketball and baseball—and reflecting on the ways faith brings meaning and purpose to everyday life. *Why Not God?* grew out of his desire to help others find clarity and hope through an honest exploration of belief.

If you're interested in having Charlie preach at your church or speak to your group or organization, you can contact him at emeraldlakebooks.com/mastroni.

For more great books, please visit us at
emeraldlakebooks.com

EMERALD LAKE
BOOKS
Sherman, Connecticut

www.ingramcontent.com/pod-product-compliance
Lightning Source LLC
Chambersburg PA
CBHW032226050726
47591CB00001B/278